REMARKABLE

→ ARIZONA ←

WOMEN

THIRD EDITION

WYNNE BROWN

TWODOT®

ESSEX, CONNECTICUT
HELENA, MONTANA

*Dedicated to my remarkable grandmother,
Wynne Byard Fooshee, who taught me
to look at Art, to listen to Nature,
and to see and hear Language*

——•●•——

A · TWODOT® · BOOK

An imprint of Globe Pequot, the trade division of
The Rowman & Littlefield Publishing Group, Inc.
4501 Forbes Blvd., Ste. 200
Lanham, MD 20706
www.rowman.com

Distributed by NATIONAL BOOK NETWORK

British Library Cataloguing in Publication Information available

Library of Congress Cataloging-in-Publication Data

Names: Brown, Wynne L., author.
Title: Remarkable Arizona women / Wynne Brown.
Description: Third edition. | Guilford, Connecticut ; Helena, Montana : TwoDot, an
    imprint of Globe Pequot, [2022] | Includes bibliographical references and index.
Identifiers: LCCN 2022027258 (print) | LCCN 2022027259 (ebook) | ISBN
    9781493066865 (paperback) | ISBN 9781493066872 (epub)
Subjects: LCSH: Women--Arizona--History. | Women--Arizona--Biography. | LCGFT:
    Biographies.
Classification: LCC CT3262.A6 B77 2022 (print) | LCC CT3262.A6 (ebook) | DDC
    920.7209791--dc23/eng/20220707
LC record available at https://lccn.loc.gov/2022027258
LC ebook record available at https://lccn.loc.gov/2022027259

∞™ The paper used in this publication meets the minimum requirements of American
National Standard for Information Sciences—Permanence of Paper for Printed Library
Materials, ANSI/NISO Z39.48-1992.

CONTENTS

ACKNOWLEDGMENTS

———•●•———

Tucson is a town rich in both writers and readers, and I've been fortunate to lean on many of them. I'm even more aware of why historians count archivists and librarians as their best friends, and why every writer needs people who are willing to ask, "So, how's the book coming along?" Even better are those friends who actually listen to the answer—over and over again.

Not one of the three editions of this book could have happened without the assistance, friendship, and support of the following people:

Arizona Historical Foundation; all the staff of the Arizona Historical Society–Tucson; Vera Marie Badertscher; Edward Ban; Hedley Bond; Carol Brooks, Arizona Historical Society–Yuma; Sinclair Browning; Rosemary Clark, Wickenburg Public Library; Jan Cleere; Rita Cantu and Al Carter; Cochise County Historical Society, Douglas; Jane Candia Coleman; Lori Davisson; Desert Caballeros Western Museum, Wickenburg; Kay Ellerman and Pat Foley, Mohave Museum of History and Art; Jane Eppinga; Peter and Frances Grill; Don Langlois, Arizona State Library, Archives and Public Records; Judy Lee; Jan Lo Vecchio; Patricia Preciado Martin; Susan Cummins Miller; Patricia A. Neal; Jim Nyrehn; Vanessa Olsen; Dave Peterson; Sativa Peterson, State of Arizona Research Library; Anthony Pratcher II; Patty Rickard; Sharon and Darrow Richins and other members of Beckie Richardson's family; Don and Lillian Sayner; Lorri Carlsson and Jody Drake, Sharlot Hall Museum; Win Bundy, Singing Winds Bookstore; Sisters of St. Joseph of Carondelet, including Sister Alberta Cammack, CSJ, "semi-retired" archivist for St. Mary's Hospital, Tucson, Sister Anne Clark, archivist Sisters of St. Joseph of Carondelet, Albany, Sister Patricia Rose Shanahan, CSJ, Los Angeles, and Sister Charline Sullivan, CSJ, archivist at St. Louis Province; Carol Simon; Wendy Ross Sizer; Bill Steen; H.

Henrietta Stockel; Kathleen Talbott, Portal, Arizona, branch of Cochise County Library; Mike Tom; University of Arizona Special Collections; Luis Urrea; Mike Van Buskirk; Jannelle Weakly, Arizona State Museum Photographic Collections; Matthew C. Whitaker; Jeanne Williams; and Heidi Vanderbilt.

In the first edition, editor Charlene Patterson was a stalwart defender of writers' rights and provided an ideal mix of guidance, reassurance, cheerleading, and patient hand-holding. In the second, editor Erin Turner was supportive and enthusiastic. And in this third edition, I'm especially grateful to Sarah Parke for being so patient, persistent, and responsive.

My thanks to all!

INTRODUCTION

As time went by, I also realized that the particular place I'd chosen was less important than the fact that I'd chosen a place and focused my life around it. Although the island has take on great signifi-cance for me, it's no more inherently beautiful or meaningful than any other place on earth. What makes a place special is the way it buries itself inside the heart, not whether it's flat or rugged, rich or austere, wet or arid, gentle or harsh, warm or cold, wild or tame. Every place, like every person, is elevated by the love and respect shown toward it, and by the way in which its bounty is received.

RICHARD NELSON, *THE ISLAND WITHIN*, 1989

I am not a native Arizonan.

But as soon as I arrived, in an elderly Volkswagen bus on a searingly hot June day in 1971, I recognized immediately that I'd come Home. A few years and one graduate degree later, I reluctantly moved away.

I spent the next quarter-century realizing how deeply Arizona had buried itself into my own heart. In 2000, I returned—with no plans to live anywhere else ever again.

Even the 2011 Horseshoe 2 forest fire that devastated the Chirica-hua Mountains around my home did nothing to shake that resolve.

Writing the first edition of this book was both a review and an explo-ration of the state's history. It was also a way to set my anchor in this particular island of the world. One goal was to bring Arizona's narrative to life through the experiences of its women. I thought my task would be an easy one—after all, how many remarkable women, born before 1900, could there have been?

Many, it turns out. My long list, which is still growing, includes more than 120 worthy candidates, and this project's greatest challenge was choosing the final candidates. Diversity was a primary consideration, not just in the women's ethnicity, but also their occupations and geographic locations.

But more than showing a wide range of women, I wanted to give voice to some whose stories have rarely, if ever, been told. Often, these individuals left no words of their own, only silent accomplishments. Thus, only a few of the women here are well-known.

This third edition allows me to introduce three more women whose stories have not been told before. The experiences of Laura Kerman, a Tohono O'odham seed saver; Sara Plummer Lemmon, nineteenth-century botanist and artist; and Ayra Elberta Hammonds Hackett, the only African American female newspaper owner in Arizona all fill in gaps in the previous edition's narrative.

My hope for this book is that readers will come away with an emotional, as well as an intellectual, sense of Arizona's history. I hope they'll know the Apaches' despair through Lozen's battles against the tribe's enemies. I hope they'll feel the noonday heat in the surgery theater in Sister Fidelia McMahon's hospital and the healing touch of Teresa Urrea. I hope they'll savor the saturated hues of Northern Arizona through the words of Sharlot Hall and the painterly eye of Mary-Russell Colton. And I hope they'll sense the profound effect of Mexico through the musical art of Luisa Ronstadt Espinel and see the often-forgotten Chinese experience through the life and photographic lens of Carmen Ban Lee. And, of course, there's stagecoach robber Pearl Hart—how many other states can claim their own Lady Road Agent?

These and the other women in the book are all remarkable, as are the many I didn't include.

Arizona has certainly been elevated by their bounty.

Lozen

(183?–1889)

"A SHIELD TO HER PEOPLE"

A few stars still glimmered and blinked as salmon brushstrokes streaked across the eastern sky. The fall rains had brought a good spring to southern Arizona. The desert willows were bright with flowers, and the yucca blooms stood tall, like white waxed beacons among the mesquites. A coyote yipped, another answered.

The horses were clustered near camp. One stood apart, watching, listening, an equine sentinel, while the others dozed.

Only one human stirred. A slight young woman unwrapped herself from her blanket and walked silently to higher ground. She extended her arms, threw her head back, and sang, while turning slowly in a circle:

Upon this earth
On which we live
Ussen has Power.
This Power He grants me
For locating the Enemy.
I search for that Enemy
Which only Ussen, Creator of Life
Can reveal to me.

This morning, her palms were cool and remained the color of normal flesh. She was relieved. All too often lately, her hands turned hot, purple even—and always when facing the approaching foe.

She didn't understand this ability of her body to locate the enemy, but it wasn't her role to understand or question. Her role was to protect her People.

The sun edged over the distant lavender mountains. People stirred in the camp below her.

Lozen walked back down the hill to let them know they were safe.

For now.

⁋

Lozen, an Apache warrior, scout, and medicine woman, is almost as much of a challenge for contemporary historians as she was for nineteenth-century soldiers. Not only did the Apaches leave no written record of her, but the white men of the time were unable to imagine that any woman could have held as powerful and vital a role—so they never mentioned her.

Some experts believe that Lozen's role has been magnified beyond reality to the point of making her a myth. Other sources say the Apaches deliberately underplayed Lozen's importance as a way to protect her. The records that do exist are oral—historians' interviews of adult Apaches recalling their childhoods spent with the famous chiefs, Geronimo, Cochise, Victorio, and others. Again and again these eyewitnesses mention Lozen. One, James Kaywaykla, wrote that the last free Apaches would have been captured years earlier except for her ability to locate the enemy. He remembers Chief Victorio saying, "Lozen is as my right hand. Strong as a man, braver than most, and cunning in strategy, Lozen is a shield to her people."

One historian points out that Kaywaykla was only three or four and questions if he could have remembered these words—while another says Lozen can claim the title of "America's greatest guerilla fighter."

What is clear is that Lozen's story roams over more than just the Arizona Territory. The Apache tribe is usually divided into six groups: Western, Chiricahua (pronounced cheer-ee-kah-wah), Mescalero, Jicarilla, Lipan, and Kiowa.

Apache prisoners in 1886. Geronimo and Naiche, front row, third and fourth from right. Historians have believed for years that the woman in the top row, third from right, is Lozen. National Archives

The Western Apaches occupied both eastern Arizona and western New Mexico and included the Warm Springs (also known as the Chihenne) and White Mountain bands. The Chiricahua lived in southwestern New Mexico, southeastern Arizona, and the adjacent Mexican states of Chihuahua and Sonora. The Mescalero still reside east of the Rio Grande in southern New Mexico.

All the Apaches were in the Southwest long before state and national boundaries. Topographical landmarks mattered far more to them than the arbitrary political lines drawn in the desert by white men. All the "Indeh" (the People) were nomadic, and they easily covered thousands of miles on horseback, often spending summers in the Arizona mountains and winters in central Mexico. The Chiricahua and Chihenne bands were closely related, often intermarried, and frequently traveled through each other's territories without acrimony.

Lozen was born into the Warm Springs band, sometime in the early 1830s, probably in southern New Mexico. The band considered Ojo Caliente, between what are now Silver City and Socorro, to be its spiritual home and where they felt closest to Ussen, the Creator of Life. It's a beautiful area of high desert with islands of mountain ranges and a surprising number of volcanic hot springs.

Not much is known of Lozen's family except that she was the younger sister of Chief Victorio, who was born in 1825.

Although the women did most of the food-gathering and cooking, Apache girls had the same training as boys: They learned to hunt, ride, and fight, since the band might need every individual for defense. There was nothing squeamish about these women: If a family member was killed, the perpetrator was caught, brought back to camp, and turned loose among the angry women, who beat, stabbed, or stoned the assailant to death.

Lozen was small in stature, but physically gifted, and soon proved to be a faster runner than most of the boys, as well as a better marksman and equestrian. She was far more interested in warrior skills than cooking, and quickly earned her name, which meant "Dexterous Horse Thief" in Apache.

A formative event in the childhoods of both Victorio and Lozen took place in the spring of 1837 and marked the beginning of animosity between the Apaches and white settlers. The Warm Springs band was lured to a fiesta by the residents of Santa Rita, in the northern Mexico state of Sonora. Led by a Kentucky bounty hunter, John James Johnson, the "party" turned into a massacre, and among those killed was the leader of the band. As a result, Mangas Coloradas (Red Sleeves) became the new Warm Springs chief.

He soon realized Lozen had a talent even more valuable than stealing horses. Since the ceremony she performed allowed her to detect enemies, he invited her to participate in raids. According to one source, only promiscuous women went with the warriors, but Lozen's responsibilities were to protect the men and fight with them. She also never married. Legend has it that the chief of an unidentified Eastern band passed through, stopping off to visit the Warm Springs camp. According to James Kaywaykla's grandmother,

> *Lozen was too young for marriage, but she had seen this chief and no other man ever interested her. She put marriage from her mind and rode beside her brother as a warrior. She lives solely to aid him and her people. And she is sacred . . . , she is respected above all living women.*

By 1861, relations between the whites and the Apaches were deteriorating fast, but Mangas Coloradas still believed that surely the land could support both cultures. He arranged a meeting to reason with the mining community in Pinos Altos, New Mexico, and planned to guide the miners to other gold-bearing sites in exchange for allowing his band to live on their ancestral lands.

He quickly lost interest in the peace process when the miners captured, tied, and whipped him before his sons could come to his rescue. That same year, the peaceful Chiricahua chief Cochise, son-in-law of Mangas Coloradas, was falsely accused of kidnapping a white child. The white soldiers reacted by killing Cochise's brother.

To both the Chiricahua and the Chihenne, war was the only honorable response. Victorio, accompanied by another Warm Springs leader, Nana, along with Lozen, led many successful raids against the white settlers. By now Lozen had proven herself on her three apprenticeship raids, and often advised Victorio about the most effective strategies. She was the only woman ever allowed in councils though she was apparently shy and said little in public.

At first it seemed as if their raids had been victorious. The soldiers marched away, and Lozen's ceremony was no longer needed. Little did the Apaches know that the soldiers were embroiled in a bigger battle and had been summoned East to fight in the Civil War.

The next summer the white men reappeared in even greater numbers, and this time they brought cannons. Lozen and her people realized what they were up against in the Battle of Apache Pass when they were forced to retreat, carrying a wounded Mangas Coloradas.

Although there's no written record, it's likely Lozen treated her chief's wound. Kaywaykla remembers Victorio extolling Lozen's ability as a healer, saying, she was "skillful in treating wounds; when I got a bullet in my shoulder she burned the thorns from a leaf of nopal [prickly pear], split it and bound the fleshy side to the wound. The next day I rode."

Six months later Mangas Coloradas realized the People could not endure much longer and resolved to meet with the white men to talk peace. Too trusting once again, he went alone to the soldiers' camp under a flag of truce. The soldiers captured him, held red-hot bayonets to his feet, shot him, cut off his head, boiled it, and sent it to Washington.

Lozen, Victorio, Nana, and the rest of the band were devastated. They hid in their home mountains, only emerging for the occasional raid or supply trip. Since the soldiers were less inclined to shoot women, sometimes Lozen was the one sent to Pinos Altos or Mesilla (now Las Cruces) to gather news.

The Apaches spent the next couple of years attending abortive peace conferences and waiting to see where the government would allow them to live. In 1870 the Chihenne moved reluctantly to Tularosa, an area they found too high, too cold, and too rocky for crops. In 1874 they were at last inexplicably allowed back to their ancestral land near Ojo Caliente, and all seemed calm for a year. But soon their allocations of stringy beef and moldy flour ran out, and the children were hungry.

In 1876 the Chiricahua were moved from their designated area in southeastern Arizona to the San Carlos reservation farther north.

When Geronimo was captured, he and his band were taken to San Carlos in chains, and the following year the Chihenne were marched there. Consolidating the reservations saved the U.S. government $25,000 for each closed reservation—but the price was in human lives. The camp was near Camp Goodwin in the marshes of the Gila River, and disease, which had already driven away the soldiers, killed many Apaches as well.

By September 1877, Victorio could stand the camp no longer and broke out, leading Lozen and three hundred warriors, women, and children back to Ojo Caliente, where they lived quietly.

Finally, it seemed as if Lozen's skills as enemy locator and warrior wouldn't be needed.

But two years later, once again the government made them move, this time to the Mescalero Reservation. In June rumors flew that Victorio was to be arrested, and, the story goes, he and Lozen chose freedom over confinement.

For the next year they remained on the move all over New Mexico, western Texas, southeastern Arizona, and into Mexico. Geronimo, having escaped from San Carlos, joined them. When ammunition ran low, Lozen and Victorio decided she should return to the Mescalero Reservation and come back with more warriors and supplies. Lozen, who always felt the women and children were her responsibility, also agreed to take a Mescalero woman and her infant back. Traveling was slow, and the two women arrived after many weeks, only to be faced with the worst possible news: Victorio had been killed in an ambush in Mexico.

Lozen was desolate—and angry. She re-joined the band, now led by Nana, in a retaliatory revenge raid throughout the Southwest with the sole goal of killing as many Mexicans as possible. They covered three thousand miles in two months, killed hundreds, won seven battles, stole two hundred head of stock—and, thanks to Lozen's skill in locating the enemy, never lost a warrior.

By 1881 many in the band were homesick for their families, and the group slipped quietly back to San Carlos. Once again, it seemed as if they'd be allowed to live in peace. But fighting broke out, this time at Cibecue. Although the Chihenne weren't blamed, Lozen and Nana feared repercussions and broke out from the reservation again, hoping to join Geronimo in his Mexican hideaway in the Sierra Madre.

Many other Apaches had the same idea, and six hundred gathered in the mountain refuge, Chiricahua, Chihenne, Mescalero, and others. They all hid in Mexico uneventfully for a year, but the war leaders grew restless, and both the need for ammunition for their American-made rifles and the desire to reunite their families grew strong. Geronimo, Nana, and Lozen decided to lead a group into Arizona and free their people from San Carlos. The raid was successful—until the U.S. soldiers followed them across the border and killed a third of those rescued.

By May 1883, morale among the survivors had sunk, and most decided to surrender, including Geronimo, who told the white men he needed a month to round up the families.

By February 1884, the band was settled back at San Carlos, but the agent in charge was unable to maintain peace between the different factions. In July 1885 Geronimo heard a rumor he was to be hanged, so he bolted—accompanied by Lozen, thirty-five warriors, and one hundred women and children. Ironically, they stopped to rest in the Chiricahua Mountains at the now-abandoned Fort Bowie, site of the Battle of Apache Pass where Mangas Coloradas was first wounded.

Again they headed for Mexico, where they hid in mountains accessible by only one narrow but easily defended trail.

By now, the Americans had hired Apache scouts, who knew the ways, trails, and hideaways of Lozen's group, and the casualties began to mount. Discouragement grew. The group had met before with General George Crook, known as Grey Fox, and trusted him to make fair decisions. They sent Lozen and another woman, Dahteste, to talk to the commander to see if a surrender was still possible. Crook agreed to meet with the leaders in March of 1886, in the Canyon de Los Embudos, eighty-six miles south of Fort Bowie.

Writer Peter Aleshire described Lozen's role in the historic meeting:

> *Lozen remained in the back of the group, not talking but keeping her rifle ready. The White Eyes had never paid much attention to her and she did not want them to pay attention to her now. The leaders hid her importance when talking to the White Eyes, partly to protect her and partly so she could continue to be their messenger and go into the soldiers' camps, counting their guns. So Lozen did not speak and Grey Fox did not bother with her because the White Eyes did not think women important.*

General Crook said the Apaches would have to be imprisoned for two years before being returned to their reservations. After many hours of talking, all the leaders, including Geronimo, decided to surrender.

During the night, Geronimo changed his mind. With him went the last of the free Chihenne: Lozen, nineteen warriors, fourteen women, and six children.

They rode hard, rarely slept, relied heavily on Lozen's ceremony, and raided from Mexico north to Tucson and back. They stole horses, rode them into the ground, cut meals from the meat, and stole more. Geronimo himself wrote in his autobiography:

> *We were reckless of our lives, because we felt every man's hand was against us. If we returned to the reservation we would be put in prison and killed; if we stayed in Mexico they would continue to send soldiers to fight us; so we gave no quarter to anyone and asked no favors.*

But the soldiers kept coming. President Grover Cleveland wanted Geronimo dead and was furious with what he saw as Crook's lenient surrender terms for the Chiricahua Apaches. The general, realizing he couldn't keep his promise to the Apaches, resigned. He was replaced by General Nelson Miles, who sent five thousand men—about a quarter of the U.S. Army—in search of the renegades.

Miles was clever, if unethical. In July 1886, he sent Lieutenant Charles Gatewood into Mexico with two of Geronimo's former colleagues to convince him to surrender. According to Gatewood's own account, he told Geronimo, "Surrender, and you will be sent to join the rest of your People in Florida, there to await the decision of the President as your final disposition. Accept these terms, or fight it out to the bitter end."

The talk went on for hours—until Gatewood broke the news that the Apaches' friends and families were already imprisoned in Florida. With that information, the will to fight went out of the warriors, and all agreed to talk to General Miles.

It was a long, sad ride from Mexico's Sierra Madre to southern Arizona's Skeleton Canyon. On September 8, 1886, the last of the renegade Apaches, including, according to some historians, the warrior Lozen, met with General Miles. He and Geronimo placed a stone on the blanket that lay between them and swore to do one another no harm.

Geronimo said, "Our treaty is made by this stone, and it will last until the stone should crumble to dust."

With those words, the free Apaches were free no more. And with those words, Lozen disappears from the record until her death. For years, historians believed one photograph of her survived: It shows her with Geronimo and the other warriors when the train, carrying the prisoners eastward, paused in Texas.

Yet her name never appeared in the roster.

The train took the last Apaches to Fort Marion, Florida. There they joined all the other bands who'd been rounded up from the reservations, even though they'd been living peacefully.

James Kaywaykla wrote:

Ours were a mountain people, and moreover, a dry land people. We were accustomed to dry heat, but in Florida the dampness and the mosquitoes took toll of us until it seemed that none would be left. Perhaps we were taken to Florida for that purpose; from our point of view, shooting would have been much less cruel.

After less than a year, the Apaches were shipped from Fort Marion to Mount Vernon Barracks, north of Mobile, Alabama. Eugene Chihuahua, son of the Chiricahua Chief Chihuahua, recalled:

We thought anything would be better than Fort Marion with its rain, mosquitoes, and malaria, but we were to find out that it was good in comparison with Mt. Vernon Barracks. We didn't know what misery was till they dumped us in those swamps. There was no place to climb or pray. If we wanted to see the sky, we had to climb a tall pine.

Half the prisoners were wiped out by hunger, disease, and heartbreak.

The woman whose power determined the course of the Apaches never again saw her beloved mountains, wide desert expanses, and vivid Southwestern skies.

Lozen caught the "coughing sickness," as tuberculosis was called, and died June 17, 1889, in Mt. Vernon, Alabama.

She lies buried in an unmarked grave.

SISTER MARY FIDELIA McMAHON

(1850–1923)

BUILDER OF SOULS, SURGICAL SUITES, AND STEAM PLANTS

Spring, along with one-hundred-degree days, came early to Tucson in 1920.

By mid-afternoon on May 25, the room was hot by anyone's definition—and especially for a seventy-year-old woman in a heavy serge habit.

Mother Fidelia was a small, stout woman, quiet but quick to smile. She watched the happy faces of those celebrating around her and resisted the unseemly urge to be proud. Fifty-three nuns crowded the huge banquet table, which was so loaded with roses that the whole room was fragrant. Other homegrown flowers perched on all available surfaces, and festoons of dark green ivy and wreaths of sweet peas hung from every possible knob and railing on both floors of the building.

A deep rumble of male voices, a surprising sound in the convent, came from the adjoining room where visiting clergy were seated for the gala meal.

Fifty years ago, the first Sisters of St. Joseph had arrived in Tucson, and today was the jubilee commemoration. All afternoon and into the evening, hundreds of Tucson residents filled the grounds to overflowing as they came to pay their respects to the nuns. As part of the celebration, the Southern Pacific Railroad band played far into the night.

Mother Fidelia had been here nearly thirty years, and in her time as superior of the hospital, St. Mary's had grown from a twelve-bed frontier clinic to a thriving health-care and teaching facility.

Sister Fidelia (No. 3) St. Mary's Hospital Archives, Tucson, Arizona

She smiled quietly to herself. God was good. Her time in Tucson and in this world would soon be over, but the hospital was in good hands.

∽

Research is always a treasure hunt, but tracing the life of a nun can be particularly challenging. Keeping letters and journals was often seen as a sign of pride or arrogance. Even at the 1920 jubilee celebration at St. Mary's Hospital, the bishop of Arizona thanked the city on behalf of the sisters because the rules of the order prohibited them from speaking of their own accomplishments.

Consequently, little is known of Bridget McMahon's childhood, except that she was born in 1850 in West Troy, New York, to Michael and Mary Combaugh McMahon. Nor is it known why Bridget chose to become a nun, but the next existing record for her is April 24, 1872, when she entered the Sisters of St. Joseph in St. Louis, Missouri, from St. Bernard Parish in Cohoes, New York. She was twenty-two.

It's clear from her accomplishments that Bridget was an independent, strong-minded young woman, and it makes sense that the Congregation of St. Joseph would have appealed to her. The organization was founded in 1690 in LePuy, France, when Father Jean Pierre Medaille, SJ, called six women together. Their mission was to live communally with God and minister to those who suffered in the community. The congregation grew until the French Revolution when five sisters were beheaded and the group was forced to disband.

The order reorganized after the revolution, and in 1836 six sisters were sent to the American frontier, to St. Louis, Missouri. There they established Carondelet, a school for the deaf, and then began to branch out around the United States. (A century and a half later, a member of the order, Sister Helen Prejean, would become known throughout the world when her book describing her experiences ministering to prisoners on death row became the movie Dead Man Walking.)

In a history of Tucson's St. Mary's Hospital and Health Center, Leo Byrne and Sister Alberta Cammack, the now-deceased archivist, described the Congregation of St. Joseph as "a religious society that emphasized individual conviction and inner strength dedicated to the service of God and of the neighbor. . . . Mediocrity was unwelcome, and each candidate was measured by whether or not she had the quality that would enable her to be chosen as Superior of the entire Congregation."

At twenty-two Bridget McMahon surely knew that she was far from mediocre, and she must have been aware of her own quick mind and copious energy. Novices were allowed to pick four names and could hope they'd be assigned one of them. Soon to be known as Sister Mary Fidelia McMahon, Bridget would serve God and her Tucson neighbors well.

In August 1872 Sister Fidelia attended the reception ceremony in St. Louis at the St. Joseph's Motherhouse. She received the habit worn by the order and made her preliminary vows. Two years later, still in St. Louis, she professed her vows to give her life to God's work.

According to the St. Louis Congregation of St. Joseph archives, she taught from 1874 to 1880. By 1880 she was teaching at St. Teresa Academy in Kansas City, Missouri, where she became assistant superior. During the next three years, she served first as superior and then directress.

In 1884 her life changed dramatically when she moved from teaching in Kansas City to St. Joseph's Academy in Tucson, never again to leave the West.

The Arizona Territory was evolving dramatically as well. The population more than doubled in the decade of the 1880s, thanks in part to the thousands of unhealthy people who poured into the area, attracted by advertising, official reports, and newspaper articles that promised vigorous living and good "health in every breeze." Indigent care became a burning issue, because military hospitals were inadequate to care for a civilian population. Early hospitals were no more than rooms rented out to patients for $1.50 per day—unless the illness was smallpox, in which case the patient was carted off to the County Pest House.

The Sisters of St. Joseph played an active role in the new territory. The first seven traveled from St. Louis to San Francisco by train, then to San Diego by boat. Next, they survived a harrowing wagon trip through the deserts and mountains of Baja California, Yuma, and Casa Grande, arriving at last to a triumphant welcome in Tucson on May 26, 1870.

They opened four schools: St. Joseph's in Tucson (1870), San Xavier del Bac (1873), Sacred Heart in Yuma (1875), and St. Theresa's in Florence (1877), in addition to establishing St. Joseph's Hospital in Prescott (1878), which in 1885 became St. Joseph's Academy.

On May 1, 1880, as Sister Fidelia was starting her first teaching job in Kansas City, the Sisters of St. Joseph opened the twelve-bed St. Mary's Hospital in Tucson and received the first eleven patients. According to Sister Aloysia Ames, author of The St. Mary's I Knew, medical complaints in the first ledger included sore feet, sore eyes, consumption, vertigo, general debility, wounds, softening of the brain, and tomahawk wounds.

At the time, Catholic sisters seemed to be the only group capable of operating hospitals without losing money, no doubt because the nuns worked so devotedly—and without a salary. They sometimes paid with their lives, and several died of tuberculosis or erysipelas, a form of streptococcus infection.

Another factor that kept Arizona's new hospital solvent was the railway: At eleven o'clock on the morning of March 20, 1880, the first train pulled into Tucson, and not long afterward, St. Mary's and the Southern Pacific Railroad reached an agreement. The sisters did what they could to provide health care, and the railway supplied an average of twenty patients a month. In an early form of employer's health insurance, each employee was docked 50 cents a month to support the hospital fund.

Some things don't change: By 1883 one newspaper writer was

already complaining that the sisters' charge of $1 per day was too high.

Although the hospital was run by Catholic sisters, no records were kept of the patients' religions. Sister Aloysia wrote:

> *This is not surprising, when we consider that in the 1881 Tucson City Directory preserved at the Arizona Pioneers' Historical Society, there is a statement by George W. Barter: "As an indication of the tolerant spirit and wholesome deficiency of prejudice in this city, we will mention that twenty-nine children of Jewish parents constantly attend the Catholic school." The Protestant population of Tucson was still small. If there were no religious prejudices there was also no room for nationality prejudices. Patients admitted to the hospital claimed nearly every nation under heaven as their homeland or nationality.*

The nuns worked long hours, caring for patients and for the orphans who lived on the grounds as well, heating water for laundry, cooking, scrubbing the floor, washing and ironing the linens by hand, growing vegetables for the table, and raising pigs as a regular source of income.

Tucson is a desert city, and one August day in 1886 a writer in the Arizona Citizen described the town's water as "a little too thick for easy navigation, and rather too thin for real estate, and totally unfit for use." Not long afterward, the city council began charging St. Mary's $10 a month for water to irrigate the farm and surrounding trees and gardens.

In 1893 Sister Fidelia McMahon took on the title of "Mother" when she was appointed superior of St. Mary's Hospital. Because none of her personal papers or letters have survived, it's only possible to guess about her transition from the world of teaching to the head of a busy frontier hospital. One secondhand picture of this energetic woman describes her as being kindly and "quiet, friendly, and methodical."

Until now, the sisters had lived across the road from the hospital in the orphanage, a multiuse building that also served as the novitiate and provincial house. Electricity had arrived in Tucson a few months earlier, but it wouldn't reach the hospital for another ten years. Once the sisters left the hospital for the day, they were out of contact—consequently, many chose not to leave the hospital at all, in case of a nighttime patient emergency.

Mother Fidelia found that arrangement unacceptable. Her first project was to commission a two-story convent, with a compact dormitory upstairs and a parlor, chapel, and two small rooms downstairs. An outdoor staircase provided access to the upper floor. The walls, made of adobe, were more than twenty inches thick—truly a blessing during Tucson's summer days.

The following year she arranged for a new two-story addition and maternity ward that doubled the size of the hospital. By now modern conveniences had worked their way westward through town. The hospital was able to rent a post office box for 50 cents a month, and in 1897 telephone service was available for $3 a month.

By 1900 the flood of sick newcomers, especially "lungers," had intensified, and St. Mary's answered the call with Arizona's first sanatorium for tubercular patients.

According to Sister Aloysia: "It is interesting to note that as late as 1915 the building contract states that the construction was 'made according to the specifications of the Mother Superior,' with no mention of an architect." The sanatorium was a two-story circular structure that surrounded a partially covered courtyard; wide doorways from each of the twenty-six rooms allowed patients to be wheeled outside for sunshine. Mother Fidelia departed from the adobe tradition and hired a talented and experienced stonecutter and builder. Seventy years later, when the building was demolished, the redwood beams were still in perfect condition.

Next she turned her attention to a facility where patients with communicable diseases could be quarantined. Epidemics of typhoid, malaria, scarlet fever, and smallpox were common in Pima County, and Mother Fidelia saw to the building of an adobe isolation cottage. It was a small, rectangular structure heated with a single fireplace, with four rooms that opened onto a wide veranda.

Her next project was to design a surgical suite that included a sterilization room, an operating theater, an emergency room—and space to tie the horses that pulled the ambulance.

Although surgeons need light, large windows are problematic in desert summers. Sister Aloysia wrote: "By noon during the summer the room was like an oven. I am reasonably certain that many an operation performed after regular hours was not a clinical emergency. The appendix was not about to rupture or the hernia about to strangulate. The room was just too hot. By waiting a couple of hours after sunset the patient and surgery team suffered less dehydration from profuse perspiration."

One can't help wondering how the nuns remained hydrated at any time of day. Their habits were heavy full-length black dense twill with skirts that were four yards wide. Over that they wore a starched coverall, and the sisters in surgery added a sterile gown as yet another layer.

Perhaps that's why Mother Fidelia, never one to rest for long, next designed a simple but ingenious ice storage facility. She arranged to have a cavern excavated that was large enough to store $100 worth of ice each month. Pipes from the well were laid in the floor under the ice, which chilled the water passing through. From then on, cold well water could be drawn anytime from a faucet to the refreshment and relief of patients, visitors, and staff alike.

One of the ironies of life in the desert is that winter nights can be as extremely cold as summer days are hot. Within a short time Mother Fidelia arranged to make the first payment of $1,000 toward the construction of a steam plant.

By 1904 Tucson's population had grown to twelve thousand, and

Pima County's population was the same size as those of New Jersey and Rhode Island combined. That year, the sisters cared for 460 patients, some of whom would stay for two to three years.

According to the Arizona Daily Citizen, by 1905 Tucson's auto population numbered twenty-five, and gasoline was 14 cents a gallon. Electricity finally arrived at the hospital, which meant a new category had to be added to the ledger: In September the light bill was $19.40.

On May 31, 1911, sorrow came into Mother Fidelia's life. Her niece, Sister Agatha McMahon, had been born in New York, and, like her aunt, joined the order. She'd made her novitiate in Los Angeles, but because her health was frail, she was sent to St. Mary's. In spite of all the best care that could be provided, she died in Tucson at the age of twenty-nine.

Six months later, Mother Fidelia took an administrative step that would propel St. Mary's from being just a hospital to becoming a full-fledged teaching institution. Because of the backbreaking amount of work, and despite the efforts of visiting sisters on loan from other schools and hospitals, it became clear to all that St. Mary's just didn't have enough trained nurses. Mother Fidelia decided to follow the example of hospitals in the East and Midwest and open a nursing school.

Part of her careful planning and preparation included a step necessary to protect the congregation from lawsuits: The Sisters of St. Joseph in Arizona formed a corporation. Interestingly, after some debate it was decided that the sisters would not be allowed to retain their titles on the document that recorded the event. The erasures are still obvious—how odd it must have been for those devout women to see their names without the word Sister.

Now in her early sixties, Mother Fidelia contracted a builder to construct a stone-and-brick nursing school according to her specifications. The facility combined bedrooms and a sleeping porch upstairs with a lecture hall and recreation lounge downstairs, all with windows that provided ample light and caught whatever breeze was available. Years later, students and patients alike said it was the coolest building on the property.

In December 1914 the School of Nursing, the only one at the time in southern Arizona, opened to the first class of four young ladies. According to the Arizona Daily Star, the sisters hosted an elaborate five-course turkey dinner to mark the occasion. The room was beautifully decorated with violets, roses, and potted plants, and the meal was followed by a musical program, and "a delightful time was enjoyed by everyone present."

The following month marked the beginning of Prohibition, and Arizona went "dry." Ironically, the absence of alcohol counted as a medical emergency because wine and whiskey were used as respiratory, circulatory, and cardiac stimulants. California wasn't yet affected by the law, so the only way St. Mary's Hospital could procure alcohol was from a deluxe Los Angeles grocer—and only then if the shipment was labeled "For the Personal Use of Mother Fidelia," which must have elicited some gentle teasing within the convent walls.

In 1920 church law changed, and for the first time, the tenure of religious superiors was limited to six years. By now Mother Fidelia was seventy and had served St. Mary's as superior for twenty-seven years.

Her life had not been an easy or pampered one. She still lived in the convent she'd had built her first year in Tucson, but since then, the staff of sisters had grown considerably, and more than twenty nuns lived in the dormitory. In 1925 a fire drew the city's attention to the sacrifices the sisters had made over the years and to their need for newer housing. Judge John H. Campbell described his visit to the convent:

> "Please forgive me, I do not mean to be rude," I said to my guide, "but do you mean to say that your Sisters have to sleep always on those hard little cots?" A nod for a reply. "And that ancient bowl

and pitcher belong to 1880, but with modern baths and running water, why is it here?" "Oh, the bath is down the hall." "One bath for twenty-five Sisters and you carry your water to the dormitory in the pitchers?"

What horrified the good judge the most was that not one of the women had her own closet. "Every woman should have at least that much privacy—every woman NEEDS the privacy of her own clothes closet," he wrote.

In September 1920, due to her increasing age, Mother Fidelia was transferred to the Provincial House in Los Angeles, where she was assigned to St. Mary's Academy as assistant superior. One of the other sisters remembers her as "a good planner and organizer; friendly, easy to talk to, alert, active and interested in all that concerned the Sisters. She was always with the group and delighted in telling stories of Arizona."

On February 2, 1923, the self-effacing but remarkably effective Sister Mary Fidelia McMahon died after a short illness. Her obituary in the Arizona Daily Star remembers "her quiet generosity, dignity, and sympathy."

She is buried in Calvary Cemetery in Los Angeles.

ELIZABETH HUDSON SMITH

(1869–1935)

HOTELIER AND ENTREPRENEUR

"The train's coming! The train's coming!"

Shrieks and giggles echoed throughout the hotel as several pairs of small feet clattered down the front steps and out the hotel's front door.

Elizabeth smiled to herself. Who needed a timetable? Children could be counted on to know when the train was pulling into town. Although she had no little ones of her own, her staff did, and she never lacked helpers to make the Hotel Vernetta's fifty beds and dust the already gleaming furniture. Of course, the enticing smell of her special chocolate cookies didn't hurt.

She paused at the maple washstand in the hallway to adjust her collar and check that her sparkling white blouse was tucked in. A slender, middle-aged, dark-skinned woman looked back from the mirror, an attractive woman who would soon be smiling and welcoming tired, hungry travelers from all over the country.

She glanced around the room to make sure the rugs were straight and the flowers fresh. Then, brushing a stray bit of fuzz from her black skirt, she followed the children down the stairs, ready to greet her guests.

⁂

Elizabeth Hudson Smith's story begins with a tale of two men: her father and her uncle. They were born into slavery on a Frankfort, Kentucky, plantation that was owned by the Young family. James, Elizabeth's uncle, escaped and fled to Springfield, Illinois, where he settled and kept the Young name. He became the head waiter at the Leland Hotel, married, had four children, and was considered a prominent member of Springfield's black community.

Sales, Elizabeth's father, made several unsuccessful attempts to escape and was sold three or four times before finally being freed at the end of the Civil War. He kept the name Hudson, the name of his last owner, and married a woman whose name, unfortunately, is lost to history.

Their daughter Elizabeth was born in Alabama in 1869.

There's some doubt as to where Elizabeth went to school after spending her childhood in South Carolina, but there's certainly no question that her education was a good one. Although some sources say she graduated from Northwestern University in Evanston, Illinois, she's not listed in the school's records. Another source claims that her father sent her to New Orleans, which might explain where she learned her fluent French—a skill that would prove valuable later on.

But in the meantime, back in Springfield, Vernetta and Henderson Smith, along with their son, William (Bill) H. Smith, and a stepson, lived across the street from James Young and his family. Vernetta took in laundry, and Henderson worked in a nearby mill. Although no definite proof exists, it seems likely that the Young and Smith families were friends, and that Elizabeth came to Springfield to visit her uncle James. It's entirely possible that she and Bill became acquainted as children.

Where or whenever that first meeting occurred, the friendship between Elizabeth Hudson and Bill Smith apparently thrived, and on September 28, 1896, they were married in Chicago. By the late nineteenth century, the railroad provided good jobs for black men as porters, loaders, cooks, and baggage clerks, and Bill found work as a Pullman porter with the Santa Fe, Prescott and Phoenix line.

Within a year the young couple decided to move to the West, and in August 1897 Elizabeth and Bill arrived in Wickenburg.

They were by no means the first African Americans to come to Arizona. Interestingly, one of the first non-Indians to arrive in the area was a black man. In the early 1500s a Spaniard, Andres Dorantes, owned a Moroccan slave whose name is variously recorded as Estevan, Estevanico, or simply Esteban. Dorantes and his slave were part of a five-hundred-man expedition to explore the New World in 1528. The expedition foundered in Florida in a quagmire of starvation, cannibalism, and Indian enslavement until no one was left but Estevan, Andres Dorantes, and two other white men. The four escaped and spent eight years wandering southwestward until they arrived in Mexico in 1536.

During their travels, the group heard rumors about the Seven Cities of Cíbola, said to be filled with gold and precious jewels. Dorantes sold his slave Estevan to Antonio de Mendoza, the viceroy of New Spain, who was much intrigued by the tales of Cíbola. In 1539 de Mendoza organized an expedition led by a priest, Fray Marcos de Niza, with Estevan as scout to find the legendary cities.

The local Indians were far from hospitable, and Estevan was killed at Háwikuh, the southernmost of the Zuni pueblos near Gallup, New Mexico. Nonetheless, his story lives on, and many writers believe a description of black history in the Southwest is incomplete without it.

Three centuries after Estevan's demise, only a tiny number of blacks had settled in the West, and very few of them were women. In fact, by 1850 there were only 392 black women west of the Mississippi, less than 1 percent of the population.

The arrival of the railroad helped change all that, and census records show that as many as 150,000 African Americans had moved to the West by 1880.

Life in the South was anything but kind, but the decision to leave was sometimes still a difficult one, especially given the frontier's reputation for being "a heaven for men and dogs but a hell for women and oxen." Many decided to remain where they were, leading one historian to postulate that "Gold Rush blacks were in many ways exceptional and represented a higher degree of initiative, aggressiveness and tenacity than most Americans, black or white."

Although many prefer to think black settlers found the western frontier safe from prejudice, that wasn't the case.

Historian William Loren Katz discussed racism on the western frontier:

> *The frontier experience furnishes ample proof of the nationalization of racial hostility. The intrepid pioneers who crossed the western plains carried the virus of racism with them, as much a part of their psyche as their heralded courage and their fears. Once settled in the frontier communities, the hearty souls erected the racial barriers their forefathers had created back east. As these pioneers cleared the land, built homes, schools, churches, and planted crops, they transplanted their bigotry into western frontier life. Even after the death of slavery, their belief in black inferiority would remain. The pioneers and their children would hold tenaciously to the creed of their forefathers.*

As the frontier expanded, so did discrimination. Historian Lawrence B. de Graaf wrote that around 1850:

> *Black women also struggled with a rising tide of social discrimination in places of business. The black press in the Los Angeles area carried frequent stories of exclusion or denial of service to blacks in the early twentieth century, and there is little reason to believe that these conditions were not typical of the status of blacks throughout the West. Restaurants outside the black community frequently refused to serve blacks, theatres refused them admission, and some department stores denied them service. They could not rent rooms in most hotels. Public recreation facilities were*

either closed to blacks, opened on a limited and segregated basis,
or separately constructed in black and white neighborhoods.

Incomplete and sometimes totally inaccurate portrayals of early African Americans didn't add to the public's general knowledge. As early as 1826 John Syme depicted the famous naturalist and artist John James Audubon as white. In actuality Audubon's sea captain father married a Haitian woman who passed her dark skin on to her son. (In a European example, the French composer Camille Saint-Saëns's face was never shown because he too was of Haitian descent and dark featured.)

But, thanks to its numerous mining camps, Wickenburg would have a multicultural settlement ready to welcome the Smiths and other black would-be residents. The town bustled with eager gold seekers, and until 1890 most of the residents were more concerned about the color of the metal underground than the color of their neighbors' skin. But an underlying divisiveness became apparent when, at two o'clock in the morning of February 22, 1890, the Walnut Grove Dam collapsed. The dam had been built two years earlier to impound water from the Bradshaw Mountains for hydraulic mining. The breach heaved the unleashed Hassayampa River into a construction camp of Mexican and Chinese workers fifteen miles downstream, killing seventy to a hundred people, more than any other dam disaster in the state's history, before or since.

Along with the sixty-two million cubic meters of rushing water, the flood carried a torrent of racial unrest to the town. In a tremendous journalistic faux pas, the newspaper reported the names of all the white individuals who died, but only mentioned the deaths of "seven Mexicans and eight Chinamen" without identifying them.

When Bill and Elizabeth Smith arrived in Wickenburg seven years later, they were able to find work at a rundown hotel called the Baxter. Elizabeth cooked and cleaned, and Bill managed the place and tended bar. They sank most of their savings into sprucing up the dilapidated adobe structure, and it wasn't long before Elizabeth's culinary skills drew people to the hotel. The Baxter began to prosper, and within a few months, Elizabeth was managing the accounts as well.

The following year Bill's mother, Vernetta, died and was buried in the Springfield, Illinois, Oak Ridge Cemetery, the same graveyard that holds Abraham Lincoln's remains.

In those days train travel was an arduous endurance event, punctuated by multiple refueling stops in tiny, dusty, forlorn towns. Rarely was there anywhere that passengers could relax, wash up, and eat a good meal. Around 1900, officials from the Santa Fe Railroad, impressed by the Baxter's success, asked Bill and Elizabeth to establish a new hotel that would be convenient to the railway station.

Although one story has it that George Pullman, founder of the Pullman Company and Bill's former boss, donated the money, it's more likely that Bill borrowed money using Vernetta's house as collateral. According to another story, Vernetta herself donated the money, but that seems unlikely because she died six years before the hotel opened. She had, however, given Bill the title to her house several years before her death.

Elizabeth hired Phoenix architect James Creighton to build the new hotel. Creighton had designed notable buildings all over the territory, including the first city hall and the Adams Hotel in Phoenix, Globe's Dominion Hotel, the Pinal County Courthouse, and Old Main, the first permanent structure on the campus of the University of Arizona in Tucson.

Like many black women, Elizabeth was a woman of deep faith. She believed that the church was a vital piece of a civilized society. She and the architect Creighton were both Presbyterians and included a large cross on the floor of the lobby to let visitors know they were not in God-forsaken territory. Several years later, the two helped establish the Community Church, which would become the First Presbyterian Church of Wickenburg.

At about this time Elizabeth must have had second thoughts about the state she'd chosen as her home. In 1901 the Arizona territorial legislature passed a bill mandating segregation. Perhaps she was glad that she and Bill had remained childless, for the law required black students to be educated separately any time more than eight lived in one school district. That law remained on the books for the next thirty-eight years.

By 1928 twenty-three black schools had been started in the state of Arizona, none of them in Wickenburg.

Elizabeth was well prepared to run a hotel, and her educational level was not unusual for a black woman of the West. Throughout the western states, African American women held fund-raisers for schools and formed literary societies. By 1860 their literacy rate was 74 percent—far higher than anywhere else in the country, or that of their white counterparts.

The new business venture, which Bill and Elizabeth named the Hotel Vernetta, became the showplace of Wickenburg. Built of red brick with walls twelve inches thick and topped with six towering chimneys, it had fifty luxurious rooms that Elizabeth advertised as "lovely, quiet and well ventilated." It was cool in summer but still comfortably warm in Wickenburg's crisp winters. The superb meals that Elizabeth prepared from vegetables grown in her garden and meat butchered on site drew diners from as far away as Phoenix.

The hotel evolved into much more than a place to stay or eat. The lobby became a local meeting place and included a post office, shoe shop, bank, and later a radio repair shop.

The officials of the railway were so pleased they commissioned a sidewalk that led straight from the station platform to the hotel's front door, thus sparing traveling ladies and their long skirts from Arizona's copious dust.

As admirable as Elizabeth's accomplishments were, she was only one of many tough-minded and talented black women who ran entrepreneurial ventures all over the American frontier. By 1900 many of the seventy hotels west of the Mississippi were managed by women, and being a hotelier was a prestigious business for black women. According to historian Katz:

On the frontier [black women] stood out as an elite breed itching to challenge first slavery, then the mold set by white male society. . . . They had to tame the wild in nature and man, but, recalled Sarah Fountain of Dearfield, Colorado, "they were that kind of women. To make a life you endure most anything, women do." Many proved as tough, spirited, and resilient as the wilderness they came to conquer.

Black women's settlement patterns were different than those of white women. Katz writes that they preferred an urban existence over a rural one. Black women tended to be older than white pioneer women (twenty to forty years old), and they were more likely to be married, well educated, and have fewer children. Census figures show that most western black women worked as midwives, house servants, nannies to white children, laundresses, or cleaners. In 1871 black troopers were assigned to Camp Verde. Quite a few black women accompanied their husbands to the military reservation and took in laundry. Morality was held in high esteem: Very few black women were prostitutes, and they also provided the social backbone for many of the western churches with black congregations.

That morality and those spiritual values were surely a frequent topic at the Smith household. The Black and Tan Saloon was part of the hotel lobby and Bill's responsibility, but sometimes it must have seemed to Elizabeth as if the bar ran him. Often the bottles were tempting enough that he vanished with several, not returning for weeks. By 1912 she'd put up with one disappearance too many and divorced him. Bill became a drifter, dying in California in 1926.

Had she wanted a second husband, she could have had her pick. Black men far outnumbered black women on the frontier to the point that the mail-order bride business was a thriving one. Married women, concerned about all those unattached men, wrote to the churches back East assuring those brave enough to make the trip of outstanding marriage candidates and good homes. Hundreds of hopeful women, both the young and the not-so-young, arrived in Arizona.

Conditions were not always ideal, as historian Barbara Richardson described them:

> *Since older, experienced miners controlled the camps, they demanded and won first choice in brides. Many men lived through several wives and were left with large families as repeated childbirths under unsanitary conditions took a high death toll among frontier women. Men old enough to be their choice's father or grandfather, picked the youngest mail-order candidates, hoping that decent instincts, strength and small miracles would produce surviving wives and successful families.*
>
> *The black mail-order brides had to labor dawn to dusk in field and home, and work at making their marriage successful with a man not of their own choosing. Often they had to rear children from previous marriages as well as their own. There was work aplenty and a wealth of children, but they were used to making something out of nothing whether it was homes, food, clothes or scraps for bedding. Their pioneer grit deserves celebration.*

But Elizabeth Smith had apparently had enough of married life, and she remained single, devoting her considerable energy instead to the hotel and her other investments. She bought a ranch, made some mining claims, and owned a dozen rental houses, in addition to a barbershop and a restaurant. She established an opera house and occasionally performed on stage herself.

She was an avid bridge player, and warm Wickenburg afternoons included the sounds of laughter and shuffling cards as foursomes played in the hotel's lobby. If indeed she did grow up in New Orleans, that background paid off, as culture-hungry Phoenicians drove fifty miles for their weekly French lessons.

Life was good for Elizabeth—until the Depression. Work was hard to find for blacks and whites. Often tough times bring out people's less attractive qualities, and the citizens of Wickenburg were no exception. Writer Jan Cleere described Elizabeth's situation as follows:

> *Citizens of Wickenburg started to view Elizabeth in a different light and eventually townspeople refused to eat in the Vernetta's dining room. Newcomers assumed she was the hotel maid. Bridge players met behind closed parlor doors, excluding Elizabeth. Racial prejudice even ousted her from the Presbyterian church she'd helped to establish years before.*
>
> *She became a stranger among old friends.*

Eventually, the only visitors were her Mexican, Asian, and other non-white friends, and she had no choice but to close the hotel.

Elizabeth Smith died in the spring of 1935, leaving an estate of $50,000, roughly equivalent to $600,000 today. People claiming to be long-lost relatives came from everywhere, but after an extensive probate battle, her estate went to the Young family.

The hotel, now an office building (and minus the chimneys), is listed on the National Register of Historic Places and still stands next to the railroad tracks.

After her death, despite her many assets and all that she'd contributed to help the town thrive, white Wickenburg turned its back on Elizabeth. The community refused to allow her to be buried in the whites-only graveyard. She lies buried in the Garcia Cemetery just outside town with the Mexicans, Indians, African Americans, and Asians who remained her friends to the end of her life.

Anna E. Durkee

(1869–1948)

MINING ENTREPRENEUR

Summer was well underway on Tuesday, June 14, 1890, and the afternoon sun beat in the windows at the Jackson, New York, schoolhouse. Miss Anna Ploss's pupils thought longingly of swimming in the nearby Chatauqua Lake—and, truth be told, a refreshing dip probably occurred to their young teacher as well.

Suddenly the school day took an unexpected turn as Constable Denslow, from the nearby town of Jamestown, knocked on the frame of the open door.

"Miss Ploss," he said, "I'm here to arrest you for grand larceny."

Anna stared at the policeman. The schoolroom burst into gasps, chatter, and exclamations.

"Children! CHILDREN!" Anna had to shout over the hubbub. "That's enough! School is dismissed for the day. Don't forget your homework!"

Constable Denslow stood aside as the children filed through the doorway in silence, then scattered in all directions at a run.

"This can't be," Anna said quietly. "What am I supposed to have stolen?"

"Mr. Price, your landlord at the boarding house, says you stole $25 in greenbacks," the constable replied. "I'm afraid you'll have to come with me."

Anna accompanied the policeman back to town and pleaded "not guilty" before the grand jury, along with posting bail.

Two days later, the local paper reported, "Miss Ploss has always borne a good reputation and there are many who believe the charges are malicious and without foundation."

Anna Durkee (center) with Mary T. Elmer (left) and A. B. Taylor (right) in Ash Fork, Arizona, circa February 1923. Mr. Taylor was secretary and treasurer of the Dardanelles Amalgamated Mines, Inc. Courtesy of the Ballou family

Whatever the source, Anna still had to live with the charges—and the resulting gossip—all summer.

Finally, in early September, the grand jury met again and found no bill against her.

∽

Being falsely accused of grand larceny was only one of the events in Anna Durkee's life that fueled her determination to be dependent on no one. She was born December 6, 1869, to Martin and Mary Ploss in Harmony, New York, and was one of three children. Her family life was chaotic and insecure: No one quite knows what happened to her birth mother, as records show that Martin was married, then divorced, and in and out of various mental institutions. Anna and her two brothers were usually left with other people, and here Anna got lucky. Martin was a farmhand and, at one point, was living on property belonging to George and Julia Durkee. (George's younger brother, Eugene, years later founded Durkee Spices and Durkee Famous Foods.)

George and Julia, who had no children of their own, liked Anna and made her part of the family when she was around six years old. Although no official adoption records have been found—nor even any that reveal her middle name!—she took on the last name of Durkee. Census records and death certificates show that Julia and Anna identified each other as mother and daughter the rest of their lives.

Anna began figuring out financial deals early. In 1888, at about sixteen, she bought 1.5 acres from Martin's second wife and leased the land back to her for $1 per year.

At eighteen, she started teaching and was employed at several local schools for the next few years. During this time, in 1893, an event occurred that she may not have known about: At the World Exposition in Chicago, Nikola Tesla demonstrated alternating current (AC), using copper as a conductor.

Eleven years later, copper would change the direction of Anna Durkee's life.

In 1895, she had another financial misadventure. The records are vague, but it seems she owed one Charles Carpenter $41.82, and the only way to pay him was to lose her only real estate: most likely, the 1.5 acres that she had leased to her stepmother.

The records are again a blank until Anna reappears in Minneapolis in 1897. Here she worked as a clerk in a dry goods store, then as a stenographer, then at the university library for two years until 1900, when she became an insurance agent for New York Life Insurance Co. She then changed jobs to work for the Pennsylvania Mutual Life Insurance Co.

In 1903, in a surprising change of interest, and perhaps a harbinger of her Arizona life, Anna became the business manager of South Dewey Mining Co. of South Dakota, whose mission was to run the Dewey Tunnel site at the Thunder Mountain gold mine. A year later, she worked as a stockbroker, still in the same New York Life building.

Although the next few years revolved around property in Alaska, they were the foundation for the effect Anna would have in Arizona.

It might have been the combination of mining and selling stock that attracted Charles E. Jury, owner of the Portage Mountain Mining Co., to Anna. Or perhaps he realized that he could benefit from this bright thirty-five-year-old woman's energy and ambition—not to mention her wealthy contacts in the university community. In January 1904, he offered her a position selling stock for Portage Mountain Mining Co.

Anna and Charles worked out an arrangement in which she would get a 33.3 percent commission on each sale. The company had a significant group of twenty-one copper claims on Kupreanof Island off the coast of southeastern Alaska. Washington State law said that state-based companies had to conduct all their business within that state. But Charles set up a mostly empty office front in Seattle while doing the company's business in his hometown of Minneapolis. This error of judgment would later work in Anna's favor.

By April 1906, much on-site initial work—clearing, assays, initial shaft tunnels on several claims—had been performed, and the company desperately needed investors.

By then, Anna had generated $73,000 for the company, and it was already clear that Charles Jury did not have her best interests in mind. Somehow he never was quite able to find the time to put her contract in writing. While in one letter, he announced that she'd been elected to be a company director, in another he told her she couldn't be a director because she didn't own any company stock.

She was distrustful enough that she began bringing along a woman friend to act as a witness during business discussions with Jury. One remembered—and testified later—that he said to Anna:

You have just got another one of those nervous spells of suspicion; but you may be assured that we are going to stand by you. But just wait until you cool off and you will see that there was nothing to get nervous about. . . . You think this over a little and you will see it in a different light.

In August 1906 Jury wanted Anna to go to Alaska and see the actual mine so that she'd be better able to sell stock. Because of a time conflict with a client, Anna and her friend Mary Elmer traveled to Alaska earlier than the rest of the company. The timing allowed Anna to do some corporate prospecting of her own, and, while there, she met Alexander Vreatt, the supervisor of a not-very-successful local garnet mine. Within weeks Anna formed a women-run company to turn it around—and did so.

On December 30, 1906, the Sunday Pioneer Press reported:

WOMEN TO RUN GARNET MINE
ORGANIZE A $1,000,000
CORPORATION
ALL BY THEMSELVES

Twin City Women of Business Experience Launch
Enterprise of Their Own, and Take Up All the
Official Jobs—Man Would Be Too Bossy
to Have Around

The Alaska Garnet Mining and Manufacturing Company, which has been incorporated with a capital stock of $1,000,000, is the first mining company in the world to have only women for officers. There is a man distantly connected with the corporation. He lives near the mine in Alaska and has been allowed to keep one sixty-fourth interest in the company, and will take all his instructions from the women officers, all of whom live in St. Paul and Minneapolis.

The reasons why men have been barred from holding any big job in the corporation was explained as follows last night by Anna E. Durkee, 21 West Langford Park Place, who is the general manager and secretary:

"Our idea in forming a woman's corporation was simply this: If we were to allow one man as the officer or director he would immediately become masterful and believe it his duty and privilege to dominate. Then another thing. A long business experience has shown me that many men who are honest with their fellows will sometimes defraud a woman."

The Pioneer Press concluded:

If the other corporations are as well equipped to conduct a corporation as Miss Durkee appears to be, the company should make as flourishing a record as any concern operated by men. All officers in the company are women of business experience, who have investigated thoroughly the possibilities of the mine in Alaska. All the stock has been subscribed for, so that there is no use of any men hanging around. Enough garnets have been taken out of the mine already to apply for the patent.

While setting up the garnet mine company, Anna Durkee filed charges against Charles Jury and the Portage Mountain Mining Co. for the astonishing amount of $77,000.

Charles Jury tried to get the case dismissed by calling the company "foreign" in Minnesota—but his decision to move all the company books and seal to Minneapolis came back to bite him.

In April 1907, the Minneapolis Journal ran the following headline:

MISS DURKEE WINS

Jury Finds That Mining
Company Should Pay
Her $6,500

Anna may not have won the $77,000 she felt she was owed, but she'd made a point.

Within two years she and Julia had moved to the Seattle area, where Anna continued to run AGM&M.

By now, Anna probably had plenty of money. The Illustrated World interviewed her, under a headline that read "A Woman That Can Run A Mine," reporting,

Miss Durkee says that the most valuable thing about the mine is a by-product made from garnet waste. "One day when I was hard at work in the laboratory with our chemist I noticed that when melted, garnets did not fuse with iron or brass, and this set me to thinking whether it wasn't possible to find some use for the waste material of which we had hundreds of thousands of tons. For months I studied and experimented and at last formulated a theory which if it proved to be practical, the chemist told me meant a fortune.

"My idea was simply this, that ground to a certain mesh, put through a secret process by a special machine made for the purpose; waste garnets would make a separating powder or parting compound, for use in foundries. This parting compound which we have patented is designed to take the place of Lycopodium, an importation from Russia which costs two thousand dollars a ton. Ours can be mined, manufactured and marketed at a good profit for five hundred dollars a ton."

By this time, the women owned enough claims that thousands of tons of the waste material were produced. In 1914 the company shipped twelve tons of garnets south.

Anna also told the Illustrated News:

It is pretty generally believed that a bunch of women can't get along together for any length of time without a lot of friction; but I want to say most emphatically that it isn't so. Fifteen of us have been closely associated for eight years now, and never once have we had any ructions in a board meeting—we've gone through some pretty strenuous times too.

In 1911, Julia died, and perhaps Anna was ready for a new challenge and different territory. By 1915 she was dividing her time between San Francisco, Pasadena, and Arizona.

Why Arizona? Maybe she was ready to go somewhere warmer than Alaska. Or perhaps garnets were the link: Northern Arizona had unusual "anthill garnets," used by the Navajo Indians as bullets in the 1800s because they believed the blood-red color would ensure a fatal wound.

Or perhaps she'd had her eye on gold since working for the South Dewey Mining Company in 1903. If so, Arizona would be a logical place for her to investigate.

In the 1500s, the Spanish, led by Francisco Vásquez de Coronado, began exploring what would become Arizona, hoping for the rumored Cíbola, Seven Cities of Gold, but soon gave up. The first gold mining occurred just west of Tucson in 1774 by the Tohono O'odham Indians under the direction of the Spanish priest Manuel Lopez.

In 1848, the Treaty of Guadalupe Hidalgo ended the Mexican War, and gave the area north of the Gila River to the United States. By 1849, every would-be miner in Arizona—and elsewhere—left wherever they were to join the California Gold Rush.

Nine years later, in 1858, Jacob Snively discovered gold about twenty miles east of Yuma on the Gila River.

In 1862, Henry Wickenburg, part of an exploration party up the Hassayampa, picked up a rock to toss at a vulture, looked at what was in his hand, and realized he was holding gold. In 1866, he sold it to some investors, creating the Vulture Mining Co.

In 1863, Arizona separated from New Mexico and became its own territory. That same year, gold was discovered in the San Francisco Mining District, an area thirty miles southwest of Kingman that includes the towns of Oatman and Gold Road. Exploration in the area remained fairly quiet until 1900 when gold was discovered in Kingman. A second rush occurred in Oatman in 1902 when Ben Taddock picked a nugget up off the road.

By the end of 1907, the year that Anna sued Charles Jury, that Gold Road mine had produced 140,625 ounces worth $2,250,000.

So Arizona would have been appealing for Anna, now in her mid-forties and well-versed in mine promotion—and keeping her ear to the ground.

At some point in 1914, she traveled to the Oatman area, for in November of 1916, the Los Angeles Times reported:

TIP GAVE HER A FORTUNE

St. Paul Woman Bought a Gold Mine and Grew Wealthy

From the St. Paul News.

"I can't see why a woman cannot run a gold mine just as well as a man," declared Miss Anna Durkee, one of the foremost women mine owners of the world, discussing her experience.

"If a man were successful in his investments as I have been, nothing would be thought of it," she continued. "But because I am

a woman there is a great commotion over it."

Miss Durkee, on a tip, purchased for an insignificant sum two years ago gold mining property near Oatman, Ariz. that today is valued in several figures.

In 1916, she incorporated the Dardanelles Mining Co. near Chloride, which was the first established Arizona mining village with the 1863 discovery of the Silver Hill mine.

That same year the Los Angeles Times reported that Anna was interested in the Tungsten Girl Mine in Ward, Colorado, and reported that the mining company "is made up of a group of eastern capitalists and is said to be well financed and able to carry on the development work for an indefinite period."

In addition, she and Mary Elmer were incorporators of the Arizona-Comstock Mining Company. And in 1917, she added the Comstock Parallel Mining Company, which lasted until 1929.

She filed claims on at least fourteen properties in the San Francisco Mining District, as well as some in the Chloride Mining District. In 1921, the Mohave County Miner and Our Mineral Wealth announced breathlessly that "the Dardanelles Mine, at Chloride, has entered a wonderful body of ore. . . . Miss Annie Durkee, who has been working on the financing of the property the past year, has been over at the mines this week and is well pleased with the big showing in the new development."

In 1922 Anna dissolved Dardanelles Mining Co. in order to reorganize a year later as Dardanelles Amalgamated Mines, Inc.

That same year the Christian Science Monitor said, under a four-column headline:

MISTRESS OF TWENTY SAYS SHE ISN'T A 'SUCCESS' YET

New York, June 20 Special Correspondence

Eighteen years ago Miss Anna E. Durkee sold life insurance; today she is a controlling factor in some 20 mining properties in Arizona and principal stockholder in the Alaska Garnet Company, a million dollar corporation, operating a garnet mine in Alaska, nine miles from Wrangell. . . .

Miss Durkee will soon leave New York for Arizona on her way to her home in California. She has spent some time here in financing her latest enterprise, a going gold and silver mine in Mohave County, Arizona. She organized a company for this venture and had it incorporated in Arizona as the Dardanelles Mining Company, of which she is business manager.

By now Anna was quite the mistress of networking: Shareholders included investors from Ohio, San Francisco, Maine, and New York. In March the newspaper described the mine as "remarkable for the fact that its ores carry no lead or zinc. Carloads of ore shipped to Hayden have returned about $8,000 each in gold and silver."

In the late 1920s, the mine deepened its main shaft to five hundred feet. Often gold and silver veins run out far from the Earth's surface. Was depth what spelled doom for the Dardanelles mine? Or national economics?

In 1929, unemployment in the United States was 3.2 percent—despite the September 29 Wall Street crash. In November New York's Bank of the United States collapsed, marking the start of the Great Depression.

For two years the Dardanelles mine remained idle.

One reason Anna's mines did well is that she chose good people. Under the direction of Edwin W. Mills, an internationally known mining engineer and 1902 Harvard graduate, in 1931 the Dardanelles Amalgamated Mines, Inc., was back in operation, running three shifts. By December, reports were that "a streak of very good ore is said to be coming in and that there is prospect of a large vein of material showing up."

Yet, in 1932, the Dardanelles company stopped operating. Nationally, unemployment was at 24.1 percent, and perhaps even Anna Durkee's promotional skills weren't enough to provide funding.

In 1936 the Alaska garnet mine also ceased production but changed its address to New York, where Anna and Mary Elmer were living. According to Patricia Neal, who has done much research on the Alaska company, the women signed the change of corporate address papers because they "wanted to make sure that the company was still recognized as a viable entity."

America entered World War II in 1941, and miners were needed for metals necessary for warfare. In 1942, the War Production Board issued Order No. L-208, closing all gold mines, including those in the Oatman and Chloride areas.

Even closed, in 1946 the Dardanelles Amalgamated Mines, Inc. property was still valued at $269,592.69. The liabilities were also considerable at $92,336.97.

Anna died April 19, 1948, at age seventy-nine in Manhattan. She is buried in Hartsdale, New York, in a plot purchased by Mary, her friend to the end.

Interestingly, in 1995, the Gold Road Mine reopened, closing in 1998, then reopened again in 2007 as the price of gold rose.

Who knows? Perhaps the Dardanelles Mine will reopen in time as well.

Anna E. Durkee would be pleased.

SHARLOT MABRIDTH HALL

(1870–1943)

TERRITORIAL HISTORIAN

The year was 1911; the place, Moenkopi Wash.

Most of the year, this tributary trickles from Monument Valley in the northeastern corner of the state, toward Tuba City, then meanders into the Painted Desert and joins the Little Colorado River, finally oozing lazily into the Grand Canyon.

But in July and August, summer rains pound the hills that feed the Moenkopi, turning the trickle into a raging torrent of mud.

The date was July 26, and two weary people stood at the water's edge. Behind them were two sturdy little gray Arabian horses, resting from pulling the wooden-wheeled Studebaker wagon. The man was Al Doyle, a Prescott pioneer and hired guide. The woman, dressed in an ankle-length skirt, long-sleeved blouse buttoned to the neck, and floppy hat, was forty-seven-year-old Sharlot Hall, the first territorial historian. Her official—and self-imposed—task was to explore and describe the area north of the Grand Canyon known as the Arizona Strip.

The travelers were only a few days into their journey, but further reconnaissance would have to wait until the flood receded. The water was so thick with mud it had to settle overnight in buckets before the horses could drink it. Grass was nonexistent, and Sharlot wondered if they should have brought more hay.

That evening she wrote in her diary:

The water roared all night and the wind blew, but not hard enough to blow away the swarms of mosquitoes. Sleeping on a sandbar has its mitigations, but sleeping on earth lately beaten solid by a

Sharlot Hall Library of Congress

mountain flood is like having a bed of iron. It didn't take me more than half the night to figure that our forefathers got up early not from any superior virtue, but because they slept on cord beds and husk mattresses, or on the floor with no more blankets than I had. Nobody had to call me in the morning and I didn't need a professor of anatomy to tell me how many bones I had.

Morning brought even more water surging down the nearby cliffs, and both humans and horses spent another uncomfortable and hungry night. The following day, the wash was still a "roaring waterfall," but Sharlot and Al found a crossing two miles upstream that looked fordable. The challenge would be getting the wagon there over steep ridges and soft sand.

Every item had to be unloaded, and the wagon hauled empty up the spine of hills. "We slipped and slid and skidded and scooted, but we landed at the bottom right side up," wrote Sharlot. "Then for hours in the broiling sun the combined expedition climbed over the hill packing the left-behind contents of the wagon up and down and reloading. There seemed to be enough stuff on the wrong side of the hill to load a battleship and the landscape ahead looked like one sand dune after another to the far side of creation."

Finally, all the canned goods, horse feed, and camera equipment were back in the wagon, and "we plunged in. At the steep opposite bank the tired horses couldn't make the pull and I scrambled over the wheel and up the muddy bank to ease them of my weight at least."

By the time the exhausted travelers pulled into Tuba City, Sharlot was more than ready for the guest room, bathtub, and supper. Before bed that night, she wrote: "The front-end of this day has gotten out of 'hollering distance' from its close."

That day was just one of seventy-five on the Arizona Strip. Sharlot's account, published in eleven newspaper installments, received much acclaim.

Few would have guessed 1911 would be the peak of her life and of her writing career.

✆

Sharlot Mabridth Hall was born October 27, 1870, in a Kansas dugout home. Her parents, each in their own way, would prove to be both her inspiration and her destruction. James Hall was a small, narrow-minded, surly man who couldn't bear to live near anyone or allow his family to have any "high-falutin" ideas—or, for that matter, any ideas at all. Adeline Boblett Hall began married life as a bright, ambitious, energetic young woman, but she soon grew tight-lipped and often ill. Sharlot, a sturdy child, adored her mother and learned to avoid arguments with her father by doing whatever chores were needed to keep the peace.

She began school at four, but two months later, the family moved to Barbour County in southern Kansas. By the time she was nine, she was a voracious reader, despite not having any formal schooling.

The Kansas years were hard ones. Decades later, Sharlot still remembered roaring prairie fires eliminating whole towns, the plagues of grasshoppers that devoured everything—including the laundry hung out to dry—droughts that seared crops, and blizzards that drove thermometers to temperatures of twenty-two degrees below zero.

No wonder Arizona was appealing. Adeline's brother had homesteaded near Prescott two years earlier, and his letters described lush grazing, moderate summers, reasonable winters, and gold.

In 1881 her parents, younger brother, uncle and aunt, and Sharlot all crammed their belongings into two wagons and headed west. Even though she'd just celebrated her eleventh birthday, her responsibility was to ride at the rear herding twenty thoroughbreds, the foundation for the new ranch stock.

Early in the trip, somewhere near Dodge City, her horse was spooked by a blowing gunnysack and threw her. The little girl landed flat on her back, cracking either her spine or hip. She was too afraid to tell the adults that she was hurt and crawled back on her horse, in agony. Never again would she be free from the pain of that injury.

Years later, Sharlot wrote: "In mid-February of 1882 I rode into Prescott on a long-legged dapple gray mare who had just left her footprints on the full length of the Santa Fe trail. We had been three months coming—three months with covered wagons and a caravan of loose horses—like Abraham and his family seeking new grazing grounds."

During the next ten years, Sharlot attended one year of school in Dewey, while helping run the family ranch and mining operations. She also watched her mother's health erode and swore she'd never marry. Her own emotions were fragile, even then, and in a poem she wrote at fifteen, she contemplated suicide.

A happier—and foreshadowing—event was the friendship she developed with the governor's retired secretary, Henry W. Fleury, who still lived in Prescott's governor's mansion. The two often exchanged books, and even as a teenager, Sharlot admired the building.

At twenty she sold her first article to a children's magazine for $4. With that grand sale she realized she could generate income for the ranch and justify her passion for reading. It was just as well—by now the pain from her spinal injury was so severe she couldn't stand or sit. She spent a year lying prone on the floor to write.

By her twenty-second birthday, she was a recognized journalist, essayist, and poet, and her work came to the attention of Samuel Putnam, a well-known freethinker. With his encouragement Sharlot too developed a secular view of the world and became an accomplished public lecturer on self-determination. Her feelings for him deepened, and she was distraught when he died accidentally from leaking gas fumes in a hotel room in 1896. Even more devastating was the news that he was accompanied by a young woman poet much like herself. Yet, she continued to mourn her lost love for years.

At about the same time that she met Samuel, another man came into her life, one who would influence her writing more than anyone else. Charles Lummis was the dapper editor of Land of Sunshine, a California promotional magazine. A mentor to numerous young writers and artists, he published many of Sharlot's stories and poems and eventually invited her to join his editorial staff. She felt she couldn't leave the ranch but commuted to Los Angeles when not occupied with ranching duties.

In 1901 Lummis asked two well-known poets to write a lead poem for his brand-new magazine, Out West. Both men missed their deadlines, so in desperation Lummis turned to his rookie staff member. Sharlot's response, written in one day, was the seven-stanza "Out West," which cemented her reputation as an outstanding poet.

In 1902 two elderly pioneering family friends died, a loss that jolted Sharlot into the realization that the old settler stories were disappearing. She resolved to do what she could to keep those memories alive and began collecting relics and writing more articles on Arizona history.

Then, in 1905 she herself helped change that history. Arizona and New Mexico were both territories when the Hamilton Bill was introduced in Congress suggesting the two join the Union as one state. (The bill was partly a power move by eastern states hoping to retain their congressional clout.) While returning to Prescott from a research trip, Sharlot learned that President Theodore Roosevelt had ordered joint statehood. She was so furious that, despite a raging cold, she sat down and in one night wrote "Arizona," perhaps her most famous poem.

Having a friend in the press helped spread the word. Dwight Heard, publisher and owner of the Arizona Republic, printed the piece as a broadside, and each member of both houses of Congress received a copy. It's not possible to measure the effect of Sharlot's poem, but "Arizona" was read into the Congressional Record, and an amendment was added to the bill making joint statehood subject to a popular referendum. Finally, in 1912 Arizona and New Mexico were admitted—as separate states.

In 1907 Sharlot was appointed bill clerk for the Council, which was the upper chamber of the Twenty-Fourth Arizona Territorial Legislature: she received $300 for two and a half months' work. Interestingly, in yet another of those events that foreshadowed her future, she helped put through the Doran Bill, establishing the Arizona Pioneers Home and locating it in Prescott.

In March 1909 William Howard Taft was inaugurated as president of the United States. One of his first acts was to appoint a new governor, Richard E. Sloan, a Prescott Republican and a good friend of Sharlot's. Within six months Governor Sloan replaced Mulford Winsor, a Democrat who'd enjoyed three months as the first territorial historian, with Sharlot. His willingness to appoint a woman was not widely popular, but one New York City lawyer, Frank Rudd, wrote to thank him and called Sharlot's appointment "a piece of clear, political courage." Newspaper writers were much intrigued because, according to the Los Angeles Times, she was "first of any woman to [hold] a territorial salaried office."

Despite the hardships of travel, the stress of ranch work, worries over her mother's health, and the relentless severity of her own pain, Sharlot loved her new job. She was being paid to do exactly what she wanted: preserve Arizona history. She wrote to one friend in 1910:

And all day long I'm so glad, so glad, so glad that God let me be an outdoor woman and love the big things. I couldn't be a tame house cat woman and spend big, sunny, glorious days giving card parties and planning dresses—though I love pretty clothes and good dinners and friends. . . . I'm not unwomanly—don't you dare think so—but God meant woman to joy [sic] in his great, clean, beautiful world—and I thank Him that He lets me see some of it not through a window pane.

During this time Adeline Hall's health was declining, and she worried that she'd never see a collection of her daughter's poems in print. Between expeditions and ranch duties, Sharlot somehow found time to compile her work, and Cactus and Pine: Songs of the Southwest was published to excellent reviews in 1910.

Sharlot didn't take time to celebrate. Originally, the three-sided area just northwest of the Grand Canyon was part of the Territory of Arizona. But in 1866 that land became a part of the new state of Nevada—an acquisition that annoyed many Arizonans. By 1911 the Utah delegates were hungrily eyeing the Arizona Strip, north of the Colorado River. After all, they argued, residents of Fredonia, Arizona, were only eight miles from Kanab, Utah—but it was a three-hundred-mile trip to their county seat at Flagstaff.

Sharlot resolved to explore and publicize the Strip's economic value so that Arizonans would fight to keep it. She and Al Doyle spent nearly all summer in deserts, floods, mountains, heat—and beauty. In early October they pulled into Kingman, and she wrote: "From a hilltop we saw the dark smoke of a puffing railroad engine and I did indeed say some prayers of gladness—for a thousand miles in a camp wagon is no joke, even when every day is filled with interest and the quest of fresh historical game."

The Arizona Strip trip was the pinnacle of Sharlot's writing career. Soon afterward, Adeline Hall died of an inoperable bleeding stomach ulcer and heart failure, a death no doubt hastened by a difficult marriage. Sharlot told a friend that her mother was the inspiration for every poem she wrote and that "Life seemed all blurred like woods blown full of smoke, the fall she died."

Adeline's ashes remained in a niche in Sharlot's bedroom wall for the next thirteen years. Ironically, in spite of her resolve to "not follow the same path of matrimonial bondage," Sharlot replaced her mother as James's caretaker.

It wasn't long before Sharlot's physical and emotional health deteriorated badly. Managing her increasingly difficult and helpless father and running the ranch on her own took more strength than she had. As one biographer, Margaret Maxwell, wrote:

Most days the old man brooded in his big easy chair in the front room, working his jaw incessantly over his quid of chewing tobacco and eyeing his silent daughter and Carlo [the hired man] suspiciously. The slightest provocation brought on an insane fury of shouted obscenities which shook the very fiber of Sharlot's being. Sleepless, tense, pained with neuralgia, overwhelmed with fatigue and depression, Sharlot found for the first time in her life that when she sat down at the typewriter no words came.

She was creatively mute for almost a decade before, slowly, returning to public life. By 1920 she was able to tell Charles Lummis: "This winter the work and isolation so got on my nerves that I had a huge battle with nervous break-down, but the worst seems past and no doubt I shall be all right. I have at last settled completely into the rut that is inevitable while father lives and shall find things easier by reason of making no effort to better them."

By 1923 she felt well enough to rejoin the Arizona Federation of Women's Clubs and was named the federation's poet. At last, words began to flow again—enough to justify a second printing of Cactus and Pine, with an additional section of new poems.

In 1924 Calvin Coolidge was elected president, and Sharlot was chosen as the elector to carry Arizona's votes to Washington. On January 22, 1925, she attended a White House reception, where, as she reported to the Tucson Citizen, "I felt like Cinderella . . . I can scarcely believe yet that I really did move forward in that long, long line—nearly four thousand people, it is said—into the storied rooms."

She wore an overdress of copper mesh, a hat adorned with cactus, and carried a matching purse. Peculiar as the outfit sounds, she assured her friend Alice Hewins that the ensemble "is really very pretty and not a bit freaky."

By now James had been diagnosed with Bright's disease, and Sharlot was forced to cut her Washington trip short because of his ill health. Like her mother, she'd spent much of her life cramped by this bitter, uneducated, mentally unstable man. In September he died, and at fifty-four she at last buried the person who had done the most to squash her creativity and ambition.

Into that same grave went Adeline's ashes.

As Sharlot prepared to sell the ranch, she looked for somewhere to store all her papers and relics. In May 1927 she asked the city of Prescott for permission to use the governor's mansion, which needed work. Within days the city council issued her a life lease, free water, electricity, and police and fire protection, and in return she agreed to spend whatever years she had left "improving and beautifying" what she then called the Old Governor's Mansion Museum.

By this time Sharlot was tired. She was still in constant pain and plagued by heart problems. Furthermore, organization was not among her talents. "Sharlot's bump of orderliness had never been strong," one of her friends was heard to comment. Grace Sparkes, a Yavapai County Chamber of Commerce official and a strong supporter of the governor's mansion renovation project, adopted Sharlot, balancing her books, managing her correspondence, and making sure her needs were met.

Two years later, one room of the mansion had been remodeled sufficiently enough to live in year-round, and Sharlot finally sold the 320-acre Orchard Ranch. (It was rented several times, then fell into disrepair and was eventually bulldozed. Today the site is a trailer park.)

Sharlot wished for a permanent, fireproof home for all her papers and other materials. Again, Grace, who was now chairman of the Yavapai

County Civil Works Administration, helped by finding funds to pay workers 50 cents an hour to build a special building near the governor's mansion to hold Sharlot's collection. In 1935 Sharlot wrote "A House of a Thousand Hands," describing the Sharlot Hall Building and the people who constructed it.

She spent the last few years of her life giving tours, speaking to school groups, and writing an occasional historical piece for the local paper.

During the Arizona Strip expedition back in 1911, Sharlot had enjoyed a rare respite from back pain. Often the terrain was slow going for the horses, and she spent many happy hours walking alone far ahead of the wagon through canyons rich in color and meadows filled with wildflowers. She carried her notebook with her and often paused to write scraps of poetry or notes about what she saw. On the first page of that diary, she wrote: "There is something better than making a living—making a life."

On April 2, 1943, the woman who indeed had made her own life despite heavy odds suffered a heart attack. Grace Sparkes signed a "Friend's Certificate," allowing Sharlot admittance into the Arizona Pioneers Home Hospital. A week later, on April 9, 1943, the state's first territorial historian died.

After Sharlot's death, the governor's mansion and associated buildings and grounds that meant so much to her were officially named the Sharlot Hall Museum.

PEARL HART

~•※•~

(1871–1935)
ARIZONA'S LADY BANDIT

According to one story, it was a hot windy Tucson day in 1928 when a taxi pulled up outside the Pima County Jail. A diminutive woman, somewhere in her mid- to late fifties, stepped out. She was neatly dressed in a freshly ironed skirt and blouse and paused to speak quietly to the driver before striding toward the jail's entrance.

The attendant asked whether he could help her, and she responded, "I want to look over your jail, and I'd like to see my old cell. I'm Pearl Hart."

Surprised but compliant, the young man guided her around the facility. When they came to her cell, she stepped in, paused, then touched the walls gently. A couple of tears slid down one wrinkled cheek. She turned and slowly walked out of the jail and back to the waiting taxi.

She was never heard from again.

✐

It's a touching story, but like so many others about Pearl Hart, firm evidence of its veracity remained elusive for decades.

By the 1890s, the Indians had been relocated to reservations, the buffalo herds had been slaughtered, and the real Wild West had vanished, leaving a mythical one in its place. Popular magazines such as *Harper's*, *Atlantic*, and *Scribner's* were filled with nostalgic western fiction by Owen Wister and Zane Grey, and in 1893 alone, Buffalo Bill's Wild West Show was seen by six million people and took in $1 million.

So, perhaps it's not surprising that when a petite woman named Pearl Hart was apprehended for holding up a stagecoach, the event

Pearl Hart Arizona Historical Society, Tucson, AHS # 28916

snared the imagination of the entire country. In a nineteenth-century version of a media circus, journalists swarmed the trial and the prison where Pearl was held. One writer, describing her stint as a miners' cook, wrote that she was "a good cook, an extremely pretty girl, and virtuous, firmly resisting the advances of the men in that boisterous camp. Her salary was generous, but most of it went to helping others."

Yet, according to another account, "She peddled her earthly charm and sparse physical attraction to the non-discriminating desires of the miners. Her abject lifestyle led to an early narcotics addiction and suggested contraction of venereal disease." She was often described as being a cigar smoker, and one contemporary journalist referred to her as a "hop fiend of insatiable appetite."

As an enthusiastic spinner of tales, Pearl herself contributed mightily to the wealth of conflicting stories.

But thanks to recently available genealogical records, John Boessenecker's 2021 biography, *Wildcat: The Untold Story of Pearl Hart, the Wild West's Most Notorious Woman Bandit*, sets much of the record straight. Born April 19, 1871, in Lindsay, Ontario, Canada, the child who would become known as Pearl Hart was named Lillie Naomi Davy. Her mother, Anna Duval Davy, was a determined, hardworking woman who fell in love with a farm laborer, Albert Davy—before realizing he was a violent alcoholic beast who would beat her and sexually abuse at least two of their daughters and eventually be convicted of raping several other young women. Even Lillie called him a "worthless wretch."

Anna Davy had nine children—Lillie was the third—and throughout their tumultuously dysfunctional lives the Davy siblings would remain fiercely protective of their mother and of one another.

Gifted in both appearance and intellect, young Lillie often dressed as a boy, quickly learning any and all survival skills. After several early teenage convictions for streetwalking, vagrancy, and burglaries, she spent two years in the Reformatory for Women in Toronto. Once released, she moved to Buffalo, where her ambitious younger sister—and best friend—Katy had opened her own bordello at age sixteen. The two of them then worked as prostitutes; it is probably during this time that Lillie took on a new name, after one of Buffalo's best-known madams.

The girls moved to Toledo, where the young woman now known as Pearl Hart met and married a piano player named Dan Bandman, who proved to be as abusive as her father. In an interview with *Cosmopolitan* years later, she told the interviewer: "I was only twenty-two years old. I was good-looking, desperate, discouraged, and ready for anything that might come. I do not care to dwell on this period of my life. . . . It is sufficient to say that I went from one city to another until some time later I arrived in Phoenix."

She left Bandman and, depending on which biographer one reads, she supported herself by singing or cooking—or by freelancing in the world's oldest profession. Dan tracked her down, and she returned to him. By now, both were opium addicts.

Pearl gave birth to a son during their first year together, and she then had a daughter while they all lived in Phoenix. When the abuse resumed, she left Dan again, sending the children to her mother in Toledo, Ohio.

In 1898, Dan found her, yet again, and convinced her to move to Tucson. "After the money I had saved had been spent, he began beating me, and I lived in hell for months," she told *Cosmopolitan*. Finally, he joined Teddy Roosevelt's Rough Riders regiment, went off to the Spanish-American War, and was no longer a part of her life.

That year, Pearl found a job in a boardinghouse near the Mammoth gold mine, on the San Pedro River, about halfway between Globe and Tucson. The work was hard, and she lived in a soggy tent on the edge of the Gila River.

In January, she met a miner named Joe Boot, a handsome, dark-haired man with a New England accent and an opulent handlebar moustache. He agreed with Pearl that life had to be easier in Globe, if they could get there—three mountain ranges lay between the two towns, and the road, narrow and nearly impassable at the best of times, had turned to clay soup during recent rains.

After several days of slogging through the mud, they eventually arrived in Globe, where Pearl found another boardinghouse job. But her streak of bad luck continued when one of the big local mines closed, and she was once again without work.

"On top of all my other troubles," she later told *Cosmopolitan*, "I got a letter just at this time saying my mother was dying and asking me to come home if I wanted to see her alive again. That letter drove me crazy. No matter what I had been, my mother had been my dearest, truest friend, and I longed to see her alive again. From what I know now, I believe I became temporarily insane."

Joe Boot invited her to help him work an old mining claim he had, and the two spent grueling days heaving picks and shovels—in vain. They struck no gold.

It's not clear which one suggested robbing the Globe stagecoach, but the idea was appealing. The route was one of the last stagecoach runs in the territory, and because it hadn't been held up in years, no shotgun rider rode along—just the driver, a cheerful man named Henry Bacon. The coach usually held a load of "drummers"— salesmen—who more than likely carried full purses.

On May 29, 1899, near Cane Springs Canyon, just south of the Dripping Springs Mountains, Bacon stopped to let the horses drink and to allow the passengers out of the coach to stretch their legs after the jolting thirty-mile trip. Before they had a chance to do so, two bandits appeared. Even on horseback, one was obviously much taller than the other.

As Pearl reported, Joe commanded the passengers and driver out of the stage and told them to "Throw up your hands!" while she, clad in a rough shirt, blue overalls, a mask, dirty cowboy hat, and boots that were too big, covered them with her .38. She dismounted and searched the stage, finding two guns.

"Really," she commented later, "I can't see why men carry revolvers because they invariably give them up at the very time they were made to be used."

Next, she searched the passengers:

I found on the fellow who was shaking the worst three hundred and ninety dollars. This fellow was trembling so I could hardly get my hand in his pockets. The other fellow, a sort of a dude, with his hair parted in the middle, tried to tell me how much he needed the money, but he yielded thirty-six dollars, a dime and two nickels. Then I searched the remaining passenger, a Chinaman. He was nearer my size and I just scared him to death. His clothes enabled me to go through him quickly. I only got five dollars, however.

Kindhearted robbers that they were, Pearl and Joe made sure each passenger had a dollar to buy dinner. She kept the driver's .45—a costly souvenir, as it later turned out—and the two bandits hightailed it for the hills. As soon as they were out of sight, Bacon unhitched one of the horses and galloped back to Globe, where he alerted the sheriff.

Once again, accounts vary wildly about the events of the next few days.

According to Pearl's version, the two bandits began a wild ride in, out, and across steep canyons and rugged desert country to confuse the officers. "I marvel that we did not lose our lives," she said later. They camped that night and the next day near Riverside.

The second night they rode hard, aiming for Benson and the railroad. Somewhere near Mammoth, they clambered "up a sandstone hill where there were many small caves, or holes, of a circular shape, not much larger than a man's body. Upon reaching this spot of safety we found it to be the home of wild or musk hogs [probably javelinas]. . . . However our peril was so great that we could not hesitate about other chances, and we selected a hole into which we could crawl. Joe started in and I followed. Of course, we had to look out for rattlesnakes, too, which made our entrance very slow."

Because they were known in the area, the pair hid out that night and the next day. Again, they rode all night, stopping to rest just after daylight.

"After this we lay down but were destined not to sleep long. About three hours after lying down, we were awakened by yelling and shooting. We sprang up and grabbed our guns, but found we were looking straight into the mouths of two gaping Winchesters in the hands of the sheriff's posse."

They were within twenty miles of the Benson railroad station, and Pearl always believed that if they had reached the station and caught the train, they'd have escaped.

The posse was headed by Pinal County Sheriff William Truman, who, on June 4, 1899, escorted the two by train to Casa Grande, then by buckboard to Florence. That jail lacked facilities for women prisoners, so Pearl was transferred to Tucson.

The first trial jury (of twelve men) listened to Pearl, who, according to some reports, wept, wrung her hands, flipped her frilly skirts, and batted her eyelashes. They handed down a "not guilty" verdict, which infuriated Judge Fletcher M. Doan. He sent Pearl and Joe back to Tucson to await a federal trial on new charges of interfering with the mail.

Reactions to the event varied. Some admired the spunky little woman, while others worried how her actions had affected the already fragile status of women. The editorial writer of the Yuma paper, the *Arizona Sentinel*, went on record saying:

> the acquittal of a female stage robber who had acknowledged her guilt in writing is not likely to do the woman much good, as she was immediately rearrested. . . . The action, which will be telegraphed all over the country, is, however, likely to do the reputation of Arizona a considerable amount of injury, as it will confirm many eastern people in the idea that the people of Arizona have a sneaking sympathy for such crimes. . . . In these days of woman's rights, the question of sex should not be allowed to play any greater part in crime that it is supposed to do in merit and achievement.

Although some accounts have Pearl claiming that she "would never consent to be tried under a law she or her sex had no voice in making, or to which a woman had no power under the law to give her consent," no evidence exists to show that she was ever an avid supporter of women's suffrage.

On October 12, 1899, Pearl enlisted the help of a trusty, an inmate named Ed Hogan, who obligingly cut a hole from the hallway into her cell wall. She crawled through it, and the pair then walked down the stairs and out to the nearby railroad yards. There they hopped an eastbound freight train. A week later, US Marshal George Scarborough apprehended the penniless couple in Deming, New Mexico, where Pearl had taken a gig in a bordello. Ironically, Scarborough had recognized her from the photographs in the *Cosmopolitan* article that had appeared several days earlier. She was returned to the Tucson jail where she was kept—more securely—until the second trial was held in November in Florence. This time the jury found the pair guilty of stealing the stagecoach driver's pistol, worth a whopping $10. Joe was sentenced to thirty years for highway robbery in Yuma's Arizona Territorial Prison—a jail with a reputation for being impossible to escape. The officers there were obviously unimpressed by Joe and described him as a "weak, morphine-depraved specimen of male mortality, without spirit and lacking intelligence and activity. It is plain that the woman was the leader of this partnership."

Pearl was assigned No. 1559 and sentenced to five years in the same jail. Her prison record describes her as Catholic, married with two children, and a woman of "intemperate" habits, addicted to both tobacco and morphine. She was five feet three inches tall, weighed one hundred pounds, and claimed a shoe size of two and a half. Her eyes were listed as gray; her hair, black.

The worst aspect of the Yuma prison was the heat, described as being so hot "the wings melt off the mosquitoes." Pearl spent her time making lace items to sell to prison visitors and reading books and magazines from the prison's well-stocked library. In addition, seven months after her incarceration, a reporter for the *Arizona Sentinel* wrote: "Pearl Hart's cussedness is manifesting itself in a more alarming direction than holding up stages. She has taken to writing poetry and is unwinding it by the yard."

She also succeeded in kicking her morphine habit, although accounts describe her as a constant smoker of cigarettes.

By 1901, Pearl's comrade in crime, Joe, had worked his way up the prison employment ladder and earned a position as the warden's personal cook. On February 6, after assiduously cleaning the kitchen, he quietly walked out through the prison gates, never to be heard from again.

After years of being the only woman at the Yuma prison, in 1902, Pearl finally had some female company. A photograph shows her accompanied by two women, fellow inmates Elena Estrada and Rosa Duran, in the women's ward. The facility, made from some steel cages and an old guardhouse, was a two-story structure consisting of two cells upstairs and an open room below. According to US Department of the Interior records, the prison still had no matrons or female officers, although the board had voted to hire a matron in 1897, at half the salary of a male guard.

Then, in the fall of 1902, another female convict appeared, this one bearing smallpox, which, thanks to quick disinfection, astonishingly didn't spread to the other inmates. But that scare may well be why, on December 15, 1902, the country woke to the surprising news that Pearl Hart was a free woman, despite having two years to go of her sentence. (No evidence supports the rumors that she'd been impregnated by either a prison guard or the governor, Alexander O. Brodie.)

The fact remains that, pertly attired in a dress and hat, and clutching a first-class ticket in her new kid gloves, Pearl left Yuma to join Katy and her mother in Kansas City—along with another sister, Amy, who was raising a boy and girl, possibly the children Pearl gave up five years earlier.

Within a year, Pearl married a good-looking stonemason named Elihu P. Keele. It was a relationship that soon foundered. In October 1904, at age thirty-three, she then married an actor, Earl Lighthawk, whose real name was Earl Meyers. In 1905, Katy's play "The Arizona Female Bandit," written with the help of her sister, now known as Lillie Lighthawk, went into production, starring none other than Katy herself—and was pretty much a flop. From then on, Arizona's lady stage robber abandoned the name Pearl Hart; Earl and Lillie named their daughter, born in May 1906, Saphronia Millie Lighthawk.

In the meantime, to no one's dismay, Albert Davy died during a drunken canoe trip, and Anna Davy married a kind, reliable man named Stephen Aldrich. Lillie, Earl, and Millie lived with them in Ellis, Kansas, for a happy three years.

In 1915, Anna Duval Davy Aldrich died, and the Lighthawks moved back to Phoenix, where Earl tried supporting the family by selling quack medicines.

Lillie and Earl's volatile marriage broke up in 1922, and Lillie moved to Hawaii, where Millie was by then happily married to a US Navy machinist and was the mother of a son and daughter. Lillie spent two serene years helping raise her grandchildren before the whole family moved back to the mainland to join Katy and several other siblings in Los Angeles.

By 1934, Lillie's heavy smoking and earlier opioid use caught up with her. She died May 9, 1935, with her daughter at her side.

She was a complicated, creative, gritty product of poverty, abuse, and familial dysfunction and is buried in Rose Hills Memorial Park in Whittier, California—under the name Lillie Naomi Meyers.

Caroline Rebecca Jacobson Richardson

(1872–1945)

SETTLER AND PLURAL WIFE

It was a hot midsummer day in northern Mexico when Latter-day Saints Beckie and Edmund Richardson left their house in Colonia Diaz. The plan was simple: drive the wagon to their Dusty Dale ranch a few miles out of town to spend the night with their oldest daughter, Annie. She and her husband Elmer had just been married in spring and now lived on the ranch to manage the livestock and dairy.

Five-year-old Elva and toddler Vernon accompanied them, and capable fourteen-year-old Madge was in charge of the house at home and her younger sisters. Baby Lamar was still in town with his wet nurse.

The parents, children, and newlyweds enjoyed supper, sang hymns together as Annie played the organ, said their evening prayers, and turned in.

Dawn had barely broken when the sound of a galloping horse roused everyone.

"Pack up!" shouted the rider, "Orders from the Church! All women and children must go—NOW!"

Years later, Beckie wrote in her autobiography,

Hastily we left the ranch to hurry to our frightened children in town. On the way we met droves of cattle and horses, hogs and chickens wandering off through the mesquite brush to begin to shift for themselves. We also had released all our own livestock.

Beckie Richardson. Courtesy of the Richardson family.

When they reached town, the streets were empty. All their neighbors were frantically packing, and Madge had made enough biscuits to "last a regiment of soldiers." The littler girls had emptied all the belongings into bedsheets.

"Much of the packing had to be done over," wrote Beckie.

We took the children into our arms and all went into the bedroom to kneel and ask God for protection and guidance in the crisis and to comfort the part of our family in Juarez. I hurried for my baby Lamar, to bathe him once more in his own home and look after his comfort as best I could before we left. I held him close to my heart and wondered how we could keep him well and fed in such a crisis. . . .

After repacking, we drove off and left all our best shoes sitting in the back yard. But this was a small item compared to all the rest we left on that fateful day, July 28, 1912.

༄

Caroline Rebecca Jacobson Richardson's story begins in Scandinavia, moves to Utah, then Arizona, then Mexico, and finally comes to rest back in Arizona. Her father, Jens (Swedish for James) Jacobson, was born in Sweden in 1834. Well-educated and trained as a horticulturist, he and his brother were said to have been the first Mormon converts in Scandinavia. He went on mission to Denmark in 1864 where he converted and baptized Anne Rasmussen, a skilled dairymaid, born February 1, 1837, to an educated and well-off family.

James and Anne fell in love—although James waited until after his mission to proclaim his affections through a letter penned by one of his fellow missionaries. They planned to sail across the Atlantic on a mail ship and be married in Salt Lake City. Upon arriving at the port with 557 other Mormons, the captain told them the paperwork would be easier if they were already man and wife, and married them on the spot.

The passengers arrived at New York on June 14, 1865, having heard the news from a passing ship that the Union Army had won America's Civil War. That very afternoon they continued their journey to Wyoming City, Nebraska. Five weeks later they were on their way to Salt Lake City, part of a crowd of four hundred people and forty-five ox teams.

What a honeymoon! James and Anne braved Indian attacks, early snowstorms, and flooded rivers, finally arriving at the Church of Jesus Christ of Latter-day Saints in Salt Lake City on November 8.

They settled in what is now Bountiful, where James planted the first orchard, and Anne gave birth to their first two children, both sons.

The Church needed families in Bear River City, a small farming community farther north, so the Jacobsons moved and, for more than a year, lived underground in rooms dug out from the riverbank.

On January 19, 1872, their first daughter, Caroline Rebecca Jacobson, was born.

Later the family moved from the dugout to a one-room house with two cellars for storing grain, vegetables, milk, meat, and fruit. Beckie described their life:

> *Drinking water was carried one-quarter mile from Bear River, up a dugway, and set in wooden buckets to settle. The furniture was very meager, consisting of a number seven Charter Oak stove, one of the first in town, a homemade table and cupboard of shelves, three or four chairs and a bench. A homemade chest held all of our clothes.*

Most other residents were Scandinavian too, and some habits from the old country lived on. Each autumn a clog-maker arrived to measure everyone for a new set of winter wooden shoes. Sometime early in the family's Bear River stay, James had been thrown from a horse and badly hurt. He couldn't work, and Beckie describes the family as poor: "I wore clogs longer than the other girls, and grew to feel ashamed of the fact. I planned to arrive early at school and remain in at recess so the other children wouldn't notice them so much."

Beckie wrote that her mother once had a green and white checked gingham dress that she wore for sixteen years. It was then remade for Eliza, Beckie's younger sister.

After several years, life became even more austere. The community realized that watering their fields made the natural alkali in the soil rise to the surface—killing the orchards and crops. The Church issued a release allowing them to move, and, because of his horticultural knowledge, James chose the Phoenix area.

In October 1884, after five months of preparing brined butter and cheese, canned milk, dried fruit, and meat for the trip, the family was ready to move. Beckie was thirteen and called it the saddest day of her young life: "I stood in the wagon and looked back as long as I could see a glimpse of anything, then sat down and cried. For years I longed to go back."

They traveled south through Salt Lake City, then were ferried across the Colorado River to climb "that most rocky of all roads," Lee's Backbone. At last,

> *We reached the Arizona desert of sand. The children who were old enough walked much of the way to lighten the load. The water barrels were fastened onto the side of the wagon above the brake blocks. One day I attempted to climb up on the barrel to steal a ride when my foot slipped under the wheel and broke my toe. How it pained! But I had to suffer in silence because the mishap was brought on through disobedience. It was a long weary trek over that desert with the same scenery day after day and not nearly enough water for ourselves or our animals. We sometimes dipped rainwater out of small basins in the rocks. I remember it all so well, even the smell of the bushes.*

After several weeks, the family arrived in Snowflake and kept traveling to settle in what was then Percheron, now called Pinedale. Although Beckie bemoaned her lack of formal education, Anne and James had taught the children well at home, and she was able to help make ends meet by teaching one winter.

Two years later the family moved to Heber, some forty miles away, where all of them, including the girls, worked sawing logs. They attended church and social events in Wilford, where Beckie caught the eye of twenty-nine-year-old Edmund Richardson. He hired her to help his wife Sadie with their three children and paid her $1 a week.

Beckie saved the money to buy clothes and wrote:

Aunt Sade made my stay profitable in other ways: she taught me to crochet five stitch lace and to use the sewing machine.

She seemed to grow to love me and eventually asked her husband to take me as his third wife. Accordingly, Edmund proposed marriage one day while I was down at the creek.

Spunky sixteen-year-old Beckie refused his proposal, letting him know that "I did not care to tie myself to him, since he would be leaving again for a mission."

Polygamy, or as the LDS prefer to call it, plural or celestial marriage, was authorized by Joseph Smith Jr., the founder of the Church. He called it "the most holy and important doctrine ever revealed to man," and many Saints believed plural marriage to be a command from God.

Not all Mormon women considered the custom good—or easy. Years later, Sadie told Beckie's daughter, "If anyone in this world thinks plural marriage is not a trial, they are wrong."

Beckie disagreed, saying, "I want to testify that I have been happy and blessed as a polygamist wife. . . . Any sacrifice we made for each other was rewarded tenfold. . . . We learned to worship together, sorrow together, play and rejoice together, to unselfishly pool all our resources for the good of the family."

Growing harassment of Mormons was just one aspect of an increasingly difficult Arizona life for the family. Overgrazing and erosion, feuding between sheepmen and cattlemen, robberies, and outlaws were all on the rise. As a result, the Church worked out an arrangement with President Porfirio Díaz of Mexico to allow colonies to settle in the state of Chihuahua.

In January 1887, the Jacobsons and Richardsons again left their gardens and orchards behind, and moved to Colonia Diaz, about twenty miles south of Columbus, New Mexico.

That same year marked the passing of the anti-polygamy Edmunds-Tucker Act, which disincorporated the Church, authorized seizing of its assets, and refused statehood to Utah. It also made any non-publically recorded, or secret, marriage a felony.

The family had barely arrived when an earthquake hit. Beckie's daughter, Annie, described in her book, Heartbeats of Colonia Diaz, a neighbor trying to rescue "the swaying clock and nervous furniture."

Worse yet, that summer Anne Jacobson ran to chase cattle out of the corn, suffered a sunstroke, and died July 1. Beckie's little sister, Serepta Jacobson, was so devastated she became ill, which in turn exhausted the grieving James until he too was bedridden. Then Beckie's brother became sick with the "quinsy," (tonsillitis), so she and Eliza had four patients to care for while living in tents in the Mexico summer heat and monsoonal storms.

Serepta lingered until November, when she too died.

By now, Beckie had reconsidered Edmund's proposal.

[I]n some way Aunt Sade had detected my true feelings. She wrote him that she thought I had changed my mind. However, when he got home his pride forbade him to ask a second time and his

reason considered the issue closed. But at a community dance he overheard an old Danishman say as I danced by, "Dot Beckie! She vill make some man some vonderful vife!" Edmund's jealousy grew stronger than his pride and when he proposed a second time, I readily accepted. Throughout our lives together, he often teased me by saying with a twinkle in his eye, "Dot Beckie!"

They were married in Colonia Juarez on January 19, 1889, Beckie's seventeenth birthday.

Beckie was Edmund's third wife; he would later marry a fourth, and the second had remained in Snowflake when the rest of the family moved to Mexico. Beckie wrote about her first sister wife:

I thought as much of Aunt Sade as any sister I had and my own mother couldn't have been better to me. When I was sick she cooked extra dainties for me and always helped me with my sewing. Eventually Edmund provided me with a home of my own, but we lived close to each other many times throughout our lives.

Beckie's first child, Annie, was born prematurely in November 1889, and was so tiny she was told years later she could have been put in a quart cup. Beckie didn't have enough milk to nurse her, but since Sadie's son was born around the same time, "Aunt Sadie nursed Annie and loved her like her own."

The following year the 1890 Manifesto moved to abolish polygamy by forbidding any new plural marriages. Wilford Woodruff, the Church President, explained, "[t]his Manifesto only refers to future marriages, and does not affect past conditions. I did not, I could not, and would not promise that you would desert your wives and children. This you cannot do in honor."

Over the next nine years, Beckie gave birth to seven children. Three of those died: Her first son, Mannon, was a "blue" baby who lived just one day, her fifth daughter died of pneumonia at three weeks, and, at four and a half years old, her third daughter, Stella, died of diphtheria. Beckie was heartbroken:

She won the hearts of everyone by her shy, lovable ways. Her little ringlets were so sweet, and it was the joy of my life to comb them. After a sick spell I had to cut them off, but I preserved every one and often cried over them after she was gone.

Edmund had built Beckie a small house just across the orchard from Sadie's, where she relished her gardens and transformed boxes into useful and attractive items with newspapers and calico. She didn't mind carrying her house water from Sadie's for several years.

In 1884, after her fourth child, Beckie moved to Edmund's gristmill and lived there intermittently for several years. Her granddaughter, Enola Mangelson, described her mother's life:

The children made their own recreation. There was playing in the piles of bran from the products of the mill, bathing in the water of the millrace, hunting duck eggs, playing with the brothers and sisters in her own and in the other families of her father.

In 1900 Edmund bought a large tract of land three miles from Colonia Diaz and named the new ranch Dusty Dale, and Beckie moved again to live in the granary with her children. In April 1904, the whole family was thrilled by the birth of Ervil, the first son since Mannon's death. Annie said he was "in a kingdom of love worshipped by seven adoring females." Two years later, Elva was born—named for the Danish word for eleven, as she was Beckie's eleventh child.

Imagine the torment Beckie felt when:

*Five months later, just seven days after Christmas, my beautiful three
and one-half year old son with the golden curls was taken in death
as a result of blood poisoning from a thorn wound. I was shattered!*

A year later, as the perfect Christmas gift, Vernon was born December 25, 1908. Three years later, Beckie delivered another son, Lamar.

In the meantime, Francisco Madero had ended Porfirio Díaz's thirty-one-year career as Mexican president with the help of Emiliano Zapata and Pancho Villa. The new alliance didn't last long, and by 1912, revolution, along with attacks and looting, was everywhere.

Dawn of July 28, 1912, brought the Exodus. All Colonia Diaz Mormons had three hours to pack what they could and flee twenty miles north to the United States. Edmund had been managing the Corner Ranch just across the border, and everyone stopped there for the night. In case the refugees hadn't been through enough, while they were preparing supper over campfires, the skies opened and a deluge washed away their meal, utensils, trunks, and even their pillows.

A similar storm assaulted them the next day.

They kept going to Hachita, New Mexico, where U.S. President William Taft authorized army tents and supplies. Edmund had brought a stove—the only one in camp—and Beckie "baked bread for everyone I could. The oven was filled with bread practically twenty-four hours a day."

Eventually Baby Lamar's wet nurse had to leave the camp, and he deteriorated rapidly: "His eyes swelled up until they were like apples sitting on his cheeks," wrote Beckie. Once the family moved out of the tents and into temporary housing on Corner Ranch, he improved. But he

*has never been well and strong as my other children had been
after they were old enough to eat. The Exodus took a greater toll*

from Lamar than any of the rest of us. I am sure that if we had remained in Mexico, Lamar would have been as well as could be. He has never married, but had earned a place in our love, and his patience and suffering have been a factor in making unity in our family.

Years later, Beckie, no stranger to sorrow, said good-bye to yet another of her children, when in 1938, Lamar was moved to the State Mental Hospital in Phoenix.

By 1914, Edmund wanted the children in high school at the Gila Academy (now Eastern Arizona College, Arizona's oldest community college) in Thatcher. The move—again—was grueling. Sadie's son drove one wagon while Beckie's eighteen-year-old daughter Lenore drove the second. Not only was Beckie pregnant and night-blind, but two calves sick with dysentery had to travel in the wagon with the women—bawling and kicking the entire way.

The day after they arrived in Safford, ten-pound Ivan was born.

A week after her forty-sixth birthday, Beckie gave birth for the last time. Nelma was her fifteenth child and Edmund's thirty-fifth. Edmund had purchased a house in Thatcher for her; he was teaching twenty miles away and hitch-hiked home for weekends.

Although life was easier, Beckie still worked hard: "[D]uring the dozen or more years in this location, I took in home laundry which I did by hand, often doing two washings a day."

In 1925, Edmund had a flare-up of "his old trouble," prostatitis, and was told he had to have an operation in California or else wouldn't live another year. The surgery went badly, and he came home to recover. The house had nowhere cool for him to recuperate, so the family made a willow shade outside the window and little Nelma fanned him while the sister wives sprinkled water on the sheets and tried to feed him.

He died August 7.

"With his passing, the light of the world seemed to go out, leaving me in darkness," Beckie wrote.

She spent the remainder of her life doing Temple work for the Church and being available to her children and grandchildren. In 1945 she had pneumonia and died in Safford on December 3 at age seventy-three.

Beckie's fourth sister wife, Daisie Stout Richardson, wrote in tribute:

I do love you, Sister Beckie. I love your children who are more endearing than ever. I am glad to have associated with a woman of your faith and integrity. I love the principle of plural marriage and hope that in the eternities I shall be found worthy to associate with such as you. To me you are worthy of all the honors and blessings of our Father's kingdom.

TERESA URREA

(1873–1906)

HEALING SAINT OF CABORA

The ranch, nestled in the Mexican state of Sonora, near the coastal city of Guaymas, was peaceful that morning. Butterflies darted among the crimson bougainvillea that climbed each corner of the veranda, and bright red geraniums outlined the front steps. Thrushes, canaries, and parakeets all twittered and sang in cages hung from the roof beams.

An elderly woman dozed in a wooden straight-backed chair by the kitchen door.

The morning's serenity was shattered as a child ran up onto the porch, shouting, "Huila! Huila! Come quickly!"

Although the old woman was in charge of the household's domestic staff, her most crucial role was as curandera, or healer. Hundreds of people lived and worked on the ranch, and her skills were often needed.

She hurried after the child, her crutch leaving round prints in the dust, only to be erased by her long skirt. Near the corrals, a young horse had thrown one of the ranch cowboys, and the man writhed on the ground, his face twisting in pain, his leg at an unnatural angle.

Other vaqueros hovered nearby, and Huila brusquely directed them to carry the injured man to a long dining table in the shade of the veranda. She began cleaning and investigating the injury, probing, wondering how bad this fracture was. Excruciating—shards of bone glistened where they poked through the skin of his thigh, and the man screamed at her lightest touch.

Behind Huila in the doorway stood a tall, slender young woman, dressed as befitted the daughter of a wealthy Mexican landowner:

Teresa Urrea Arizona Historical Society, Tucson, AHS # 1671

floor-length skirt, contoured blouse, heeled pumps, and stockings. Her long auburn hair was swept up in a fashionable chignon, and her expressive brown eyes watched Huila.

"Come, Teresita," said the old woman. "See if you can calm him while I work."

The young woman, ignoring the blood and dust, leaned over the injured man, took his hand in hers, and gazed into his eyes. He became silent, took a deep breath, and as he exhaled, tension seemed to melt out of his body. Huila went to work, and not once did the man flinch or cry out as she joined the shattered bones and wrapped the leg with an herb poultice.

After he was carried back to his home, the young woman went back inside the house, and Huila returned to her chair by the kitchen door, deep in thought.

"Teresita," she whispered, although no one was near enough to hear. "You have something I do not."

∽

Niña García Noña María Rebecca Chávez, known as Teresita, had not always lived in a large, elegant house. On October 15, 1873, she was born on the dirt floor of a ramada, a shelter made of brush and tree trunks, on a vast ranch near Ocoroni, in the state of Sinaloa. She was the daughter of Cayetana Chávez, an unmarried fourteen-year-old Tehueco Indian girl, and the ranch owner, Don Tomás Urrea.

Cayetana never revealed the identity of Teresita's father, but then, she didn't have to. Unlike the local Indians, Don Tomás had light skin and auburn hair, and by the time she was a toddler, so did Teresita. Mother and daughter lived with Cayetana's aunt, a fiercely bitter woman who rarely had a kind word for either her sister or "that bastard child of el patrón." Within another couple of years, Cayetana had had enough and left the ranch—alone.

Despite her mother's absence, Teresita's childhood was a happy one. Playmates were plentiful, and the solicitous cowboys watched over her and taught her to ride and to sing. She was such a merry child that no one minded that she far preferred the rough-and-tumble boy games to the more staid little-girl activities.

The 1870s were a turbulent time for the state of Sinaloa. General Porfirio Díaz had come into the office of state governor by might, not right, and installed his supporters in all the positions of power. One of his goals was to wipe out the native Indians and give all their land to the Mexican aristocracy. Being a fair man, Don Tomás Urrea made a dangerous decision: He chose to support Díaz's opponents in the 1880 election.

Díaz won, but only because he arrested and banished his opposition. Realizing he was a likely target for retaliation, Don Tomás packed up his entire estate, including dozens of families, forty bulls, several herds of cows, horses, mules, and a flock of goats, and moved out of Sinaloa to the northern state of Sonora. There he set up several cattle ranches, including a smaller one, Aquihuiquichi, and the main estate at Cabora.

Teresita and her aunt were part of the family entourage that settled at Aquihuiquichi. By the time she was thirteen, one of the vaqueros remembered her as being "tall, gangly, mostly arms and legs, not nearly as developed as most Mexican girls her age. Her complexion was fair, her eyes large and light brown, and her hair thick and long. She was healthy and exceedingly strong."

No one knows how it came about, but in 1888 Don Tomás noticed the fair-skinned, beautiful young woman and acknowledged Teresita as his daughter. Not long afterward, he arranged for her to live at the Cabora ranch.

The drastic change in lifestyle couldn't have been easy for Teresita. She had to learn to walk in tight shoes and to give up her loose, dust-covered shifts for spotless fitted bodices.

She still loved to ride, and Don Tomás gave her a chestnut horse she named Gavilán for the sparrow hawk, a nimble and athletic bird. Now that she was a lady, she was no longer allowed to ride freely, bareback and bare-legged with the vaqueros. Now she had to ride sidesaddle in a hot, billowing riding skirt, and always with an escort.

One day she slipped away to a secluded, sheltered spot on the ranch. She unsaddled Gavilán and shed her boots and stockings, let her hair down, and hopped on the horse. Don Tomás was out riding alone that morning, and William Holden, Teresita's biographer, described her father's surprise:

> [B]elow him galloped Teresita, streaking hell for leather, a vision of grace and rhythm. The horse's nose was extended, nostrils flaring, its mane and tail streaming in the wind. With her head thrown back, catching the wind in her mouth, the girl appeared to be one with her horse. She rode with her skirt pulled up almost to her thighs, the slender bare legs gripping the horse's sides. The sun caught the red glints of her long, unbound hair as it tossed in the wind behind her.

Don Tomás adored the daughter he had only recently discovered and understood her need for freedom. Instead of rebuking her, he made her promise that whenever she wanted to ride with the wind, she should tell him, and he would accompany her.

Don Tomás also saw to Teresita's education. He and his good friend Lauro Aguirre decided that, unlike most Mexican women of the time, Teresita's expertise should extend beyond household management. They taught her to read, then tutored her in history, politics, and theology. But her most valuable training came not from these two men, but from Huila, the elderly Indian woman who was healer and midwife to the local Indians. It became clear early on that Teresita too had a gift for healing: She was able to ease a woman's birth pain by putting her into a trance, and somehow her gaze acted as an anesthetic. While still in her teens, she accompanied Huila on visits to a Yaqui Indian medicine man who taught her hundreds of ways to use native plants.

Soon, she was invaluable to Huila and accompanied her all over the ranch to visit the sick.

In 1889, despite Don Tomás's best intentions to keep Teresita safe, her life almost ended when she was assaulted by a crazed miner. The trauma of the attack drove her into a seizure, then left her in a coma. After thirteen days, she died—or at least, she stopped breathing and had no pulse. Devastated, Don Tomás ordered a coffin for her.

One can only imagine the panic—and subsequent joy—when, during the wake, Teresita suddenly sat up, looked at the coffin, and demanded, "What is this?" Still in an odd trance, she predicted the coffin would be needed in three days.

Exactly three days later, Huila died and was buried in the coffin meant for Teresita.

The young woman remained in a preoccupied, semiconscious state for several months. Years later, she discussed that time in an interview with the San Francisco Examiner:

I know nothing of what I did in that time. They tell me, those who saw, that I could move about, but that they had to feed me; that I talked strange things about God and religion, and that the people came to me from all the country around, and if they were sick and crippled and I put my hands on them, they got well. Of this I remembered nothing, but when I came to myself I saw they were well.

Then when I could remember again, after those three months and eighteen days, I felt a change in me. I could still if I touched people or rubbed them, make them well. I felt in me only the wish to do good in the world.

Word spread quickly that Teresita could work miracles, and soon she was called "Santa Teresa," although she always remained uncomfortable with the title.

Don Tomás insisted he didn't believe in miracles, but he had to admit something unusual was happening. And whether he believed or not didn't matter to the thousands of pilgrims who walked, limped, or were carried through the front gates every day, clamoring to see Teresita. All those mouths needed feeding, and eventually Don Tomás dedicated the proceeds of his ranches to supporting his daughter's mission.

Although she was a devoted and devout Catholic, by 1891 the priests saw Teresita as a threat to established Catholicism. According to her great-nephew Luis Urrea, she was gently spreading the message to Indians that "God gave this land to your fathers. It does not belong to the Mexican. It is Indian land, and you cannot allow the government or church to steal it from you."

Spies and pastors alike alerted Díaz.

The final spark was ignited in a tiny but fiercely independent mountain village called Tomóchic, where Teresita had cured a warrior of a tumor at the base of his skull. The community was so grateful they made her their patron saint, drawing both the attention and the ire of the Díaz regime.

Angered by Tomóchic's actions, the government moved against Tomóchic and in 1892 wiped out the entire village. The troops then moved into Cabora, capturing Teresita and her father and hauling them off to Guaymas.

Díaz may have called her "the most dangerous girl in Mexico," but he also feared the consequences if he executed her. Instead, he deported her to the United States, with the threat of death if she tried to return. She and her father left by train May 19. Writer Luis Urrea described their trip: "All along the line to Nogales, Indian warriors appeared on foot and on horseback, and silently raised their weapons in salute as she passed."

The family set up house at El Bosque, near what is now Rio Rico, south of Tucson. Once again, pilgrims from both sides of the border flocked to her by the hundreds, and Teresita was kept busy healing the sick. After a couple of attempts on her life, possibly financed by Díaz, her father decided she was no longer safe so close to Mexico, and the family moved to Clifton in central Arizona for a few months.

In June 1896, the family moved to El Paso, Texas, just across the Rio Grande from Mexico. By now Don Tomás had become a United States citizen, and he felt more secure. Family friend Lauro Aguirre was also in El Paso. He too had been thrown out of Mexico, but he had chosen to join the revolution. He tried hard and unsuccessfully to convince Teresita to join his cause; she refused.

On August 13, 1896, Aguirre led a revolt, and several customs houses in Nogales were blown up as the revolutionaries, who called themselves the "Teresitas," shouted, "Viva La Santa de Cabora!"

Teresita was horrified because she preached nonviolence. In an open letter to the El Paso Herald on September 8, 1896, she wrote: "I have noticed with much pain that the persons who have taken up arms in Mexican territory have invoked my name in aid of the schemes they are carrying through. But I repeat I am not one who authorizes or at the same time interferes with these proceedings."

Despite her protestations, the Díaz government blamed her for the uprisings and demanded that she be extradited to Mexico for trial. A U.S. marshal visited the family and suggested they move farther from the border.

They headed back to Clifton, where she continued to heal the sick.

Teresita had always intended to marry. Years earlier, back in Cabora, she had predicted that her husband would be cruel—so cruel, in fact, that he would try to kill her.

In 1899 Teresita fell in love with Guadalupe Rodríguez, a tall and handsome miner with a kindly manner. Although the love between them seemed mutual, Don Tomás didn't approve of the relationship. One day the following June, Lupe appeared at the ranch door, rifle in hand, demanding Teresita's hand in marriage. Don Tomás chased him off the property, and Lupe left angrily, only to reappear with a justice of the peace, demanding that Teresita marry him on the spot. Don Tomás ordered Teresita to remain in the house.

Teresita, torn between the two, chose conjugal love and left the ranch with Lupe—for a marriage that only lasted a day.

A month later she described the next twelve hours with him in an interview with a woman reporter from the San Francisco Examiner:

I was married on the 22nd of June—last month—to Guadeloupe [sic] N. Rodrigues. He is Mexican. I had known him eight months. The next day after we were married he acted strangely; he tore up some things of mine, packed some of my clothes in a bundle, put it over his shoulder, and said to me, "Come with me!" The people who saw him said for me not to go, but I followed him. He walked on the railroad track. I did not know where he wanted to go, but I would follow. Then he began to run. I ran too. He had his gun and began to shoot. The people ran out and made me come back. Then they caught him. He was insane, and they put him in jail. There is where he is now.

The reporter described Teresita thus: "She came to meet me with a soft, swift, gliding step, a slender out-stretched hand, a soft-spoken Spanish greeting—a tall, slender, flat-chested, fragile, dark-skinned young woman of distinctly Spanish-Mexican type with great, beautiful, black-fringed shining brown eyes and a grave, sweet smile."

But the article's final paragraph gives more than a hint of early twentieth-century prejudice: "The glance of her beautiful brown eyes is half-sad and wholly intelligent, without any of the sleepiness or the furtive watchfulness of the ordinary Mexican or Indian, and she has in her modest, fragile person and her quiet manner such a dignity, such earnestness and sincerity and gentleness and serenity that one cannot deny her respect, even when faith is unconvinced."

Eventually, Lupe was tried, found insane, and sent to an asylum. Several years later, in her 1903 divorce statement, Teresita cited evidence that he was an agent of the Díaz government hired to either bring her back to Mexico, or if that plan failed, to kill her.

The decision to marry Lupe also cost Teresita the loving relationship she had with her father. Don Tomás never spoke to her again. Three years later, he died of typhoid and was buried at the Shannon Hill Cemetery in Clifton.

Now on her own for the first time, Teresita went to work for a medical consortium and accepted an unfortunate arrangement by which she did all the healing work and the consortium received all the money. She traveled throughout the country: New York, St. Louis, San Francisco, and Los Angeles.

Realizing how handicapped she was by her inability to speak English, she wrote a family friend, Mrs. Juana Van Order, asking for an interpreter. Mrs. Van Order sent her handsome nineteen-year-old son John, and to everyone's surprise, several months later the two were married. They settled in New York City, where Teresita healed many wealthy people who tried to give her lavish gifts in return. Much to her new husband's annoyance, she always passed the gifts on to those she felt were more in need.

In 1902 she gave birth to a daughter she named Laura, for Lauro Aguirre. When her father died the following year, she insisted that the consortium move to Los Angeles, where she ministered to the Mexicans.

But Teresita was growing tired: Her Los Angeles home had been destroyed by fire and she was pregnant again. She moved back to Clifton—without John—in 1904, in time to give birth to her second daughter,

Magdalena. She used her savings to build a two-story house that doubled as her residence and clinic. In December a storm hit, and the San Francisco River flooded the town. True to form, Teresita labored for hours side by side with the other residents, filling and stacking sandbags and pulling victims from the icy waters.

Although her life was happier now and she was surrounded once again by those who loved her, Teresita wasn't well. She lost weight, coughed often, and even her healing skills seemed diminished. Only she and her friend, the local doctor, knew she had "the lung trouble," tuberculosis, the same illness that, ironically enough, she had cured in so many others. According to her biographer, she faced reality serenely, saying only, "I feel that my commitment to the Holy Mother is now fulfilled. She does not expect more of me."

By October 1905, Teresita's health was failing. Luis Urrea finished telling his great-aunt's story:

In January of 1906 she asked a driver to take her up Shannon Hill where Don Tomás was buried in an unmarked grave. It was raining. Teresita walked through the mud until she found the grave, and stood in the cold rain, praying. She had a chill when she got home, and her family carried her to bed where she fell into a deep sleep. They mounted a death watch over her, but again she awoke. "I can't go yet," she said. "My mother is coming."

The next day, Cayetana Chávez, who had been gone for almost thirty years, inexplicably appeared at Teresita's door. They ushered her into the bedroom, where she sat on her daughter's bed and held her hand. Cayetana received Teresita's forgiveness, and they spent a joyous afternoon together. That evening, Teresita said, "Now I will go to sleep," and she died.

It was January 11, 1906. She was thirty-three years old.

C. Louise Boehringer

(1878–1956)

EDUCATOR AND JOURNALIST

Summer wasn't the only thing heating up in Yuma on May 31, 1913. It was an election day, and one of the first occasions on which voters in the youthful state of Arizona would recall one of their officials.

Louise stood, pencil in hand, gazing at the official ballot. At thirty-five she was a stout, self-possessed woman with a steadfast gaze, determined chin, and masses of thick blond hair pinned to the top of her head. Someone once described her as having a voice "that is soft and clear, yet leaves no doubt that its possessor stands firmly on the side of right. She is sustained by a native poise and dignity which put her at ease in the presence of any group or person, on the platform, or in front of a microphone."

She would need both poise and dignity, especially today.

The ballot she held explained, all too explicitly, why she and the other Yuma residents were gathering at the polls to choose a county superintendent of schools. The voters had demanded that the incumbent, John M. Hess, be recalled for the reasons set forth on the ballot:

> *He, being a husband and father, with children in the schools in Yuma, has been guilty of conduct unbecoming a husband and father and beneath the dignity of his office and calculated to demoralize the schools in the Town of Yuma; of undue familiarity with one of the female teachers of said schools, visiting her at her apartments, and carrying on an improper correspondence with her in which he addressed her: "Princess Irene," "dearest," "Ma chère."*

C. Louise Boehringer The Sun, November 26, 1919

The second column of the ballot gave John Hess a chance to defend himself. He listed the accomplishments of his tenure of office (raising the school district appropriations from $600 to $1,000, employing a better class of teachers, etc.) and added that the

Recall Petition is an infamous cowardly lie,—machination of unprincipled petty politicians for purpose of cloaking a nameless infamy . . . jealous malicious destruction of good work above set forth—to accomplish which the fair name of an innocent, defenseless girl Teacher, (one of the best in the County) was ruthlessly attacked, falsely accused of lewdness, and nameless degradation.

Louise sighed. Her pencil hovered over the ballot and its five candidates: John M. Hess, S. E. Badgley, Edwinna B. Coulter, Mabel L. K. Teufert—and C. Louise Boehringer.

If she won this election, she would be the first woman ever elected to office in the state of Arizona.

⚬⚬

Although she never publicly revealed the date of her birth, Cora Louise Boehringer was born to Jacob and Louise Greenawald Boehringer in Morrison, Illinois, in 1878. Her parents were German immigrants who had arrived in America soon after the Civil War and who spoke little English. About the time she was four, the family moved to St. Louis. A year later in 1883, Louise started school and began to learn English.

Around her tenth birthday the family moved back to Illinois, where Louise finished high school. In 1900 she graduated from Illinois Normal School, and in 1902 she earned a diploma from the Teachers College in DeKalb, Illinois, and soon became director of the Normal Department in Geneseo, Illinois, for two years. (A "normal" school was a teacher's college.)

Louise's abilities must have been evident to others because she quickly moved up the career ladder, spending a year as director of the State Normal School in Cape Girardeau, Missouri, as well as being a faculty member at the University of Missouri. When the new Missouri Normal School opened in 1907, Louise was its organizer and superintendent.

No records remain indicating what drew her to Arizona, but in 1909, when she was thirty years old, she filed a homestead claim for a forty-acre ranch in Yuma.

Soon afterward, her parents and brother George, an epileptic, moved west to live on the ranch and establish a dairy farm. For the next couple of years, Louise visited whenever she could.

After spending a year studying in New York City, on June 7, 1911, she was awarded a bachelor of science degree from Columbia University, along with a professional's diploma in elementary supervision from Teachers College.

The extra training must have paid off: In 1912 she became the superintendent of the Training School for Teachers in Springfield, Illinois.

The year 1912 was a memorable one in Arizona. Not only did the territory become the forty-eighth state, but the state constitution was amended to give women the vote. By the end of the year, Louise had resigned from her new job in Illinois and left the Midwest to move to Yuma permanently.

She soon discovered that education had had a rough start in her adopted state. The earliest settlers were far more interested in escaping either the law or the Indians than in establishing schools. By the time Anson P. K. Safford became the territory's third governor in 1869, Arizona was still a mess. In fact, on his way to take on the Indian "problem," the colorful General William Tecumseh Sherman is alleged to have growled, "We have fought one war with Mexico to acquire Arizona and we ought to have another to compel her to take it back."

The territory was in debt to the tune of $25,000, the legal system a confused shambles, and of the 1,621 school-age children listed in the 1870 census (which did not include Native Americans), only 149 were in school. Of those, 130 were girls enrolled in the Sisters of St. Joseph Academy in Tucson, and the other 19 were in various private subscription-based schools. Public schools didn't exist, and the 1870 annual report of the commissioner of education stated that: "Arizona has never had any schools worth mentioning. Numerous attempts have failed to elicit any correspondence from either officials or private citizens respecting the existence or condition of any schools in that territory."

Governor Safford was a short, earnest, well-traveled young man whose determination won over those around him. The Weekly Arizona Miner described him thus: "The Governor is little, but is, we judge, composed of the right sort of material. He is as full of vim as an egg is of meat, and will do his utmost to place the Territory in a peaceful, prosperous condition."

He, along with Mexican citizen and Tucson mayor Estevan Ochoa, changed the face of education in Arizona. In 1871 Safford wrote the first comprehensive school law, and Ochoa presented it to the legislature, which reluctantly approved it by the end of the session.

Much of that law still stands today—with the exception of one section that would affect a Miss C. Louise Boehringer four decades later.

Because he felt he was the man for the job, Safford believed the territorial governor should also be superintendent of public instruction. Another gubernatorial responsibility was to appoint the county probate judges—who were also the county school superintendents.

The first high school opened in Phoenix in 1885. By the time Louise moved to Yuma in 1912, the state's school-age population had mushroomed to 42,318, and male teachers were paid $81 per month, while female teachers received $65 per month.

Years later, the editor of an eastern newspaper was impressed by "Miss Boehringer":

She soon discovered that educational facilities were sadly lacking in that section. She called a county meeting to consider the school situation. But the unmarried ranchmen were not interested in schools. They wanted better roads and Miss Boehringer saw her school meeting transformed into a good roads conference.

She allied herself with the young ranchmen and they in turn helped her to secure better schools. Later these same men helped the women to elect Miss Boehringer county superintendent under dramatic circumstances.

Part of those dramatic circumstances revolved around Arizona's contested statehood. The draft of the constitution sent to Washington for President Taft's signature included a provision allowing the new state to recall all officials, including judges. Taft was opposed to the idea and vetoed the whole constitution. So, the determined Arizonans sent the proposed constitution back without the provision and celebrated wildly on February 14, 1912, when Arizona was officially declared a state.

They promptly amended their new constitution to reinsert the recall option.

In the same year residents of Yuma County, horrified by the "unbecoming" behavior of John Hess, the incumbent county superintendent, initiated a move to recall him. The Arizona Supreme Court used the new constitution to rule that the recall election was legal.

Although she hadn't been a full-time state resident for long, Louise was invited to run against Hess and against three other female candidates. She won decisively, becoming the first woman elected to office in the new state of Arizona. She served four years as county superintendent of schools (1913–1917).

By now she was also editor of the Arizona Teacher, and in the October 1915 issue, she encouraged all teachers to continue their growth and development to make "'it possible to keep the work of the classroom more closely related to the problems and interests of life.'"

Apparently, teacher burnout is not a recent phenomenon. In the same editorial she offered the following advice:

> *That the social and play side of the teacher should be nourished is essential. Teachers who keep alive the play spirit have more power with the active, restless boy and girl because they have so much in common. Teachers should make provision for their own recreation and play just as they do for their study and work, in order that they may remain youthful and vigorous, and sympathetic with all that is a part of the life of active, playful boys and girls.*

Louise also recognized the need for networking, and in 1915 she set up the State Council of Administrative Women in Education for principals, high school department heads, and other county superintendents, serving as its first president. In 1925 she was unanimously elected president again—even though she'd already held that position during the entire existence of the organization.

In 1916 she ran for state superintendent of public instruction but was defeated. This officer oversees the work of the State Department of Education, and it was a position that Louise apparently longed for but never won.

She spent the next summer studying journalism at the University of Illinois, and, when she returned to Yuma in the fall, she bought the Arizona Teacher. She would spend the next twenty-two years publishing (and occasionally financing) 264 issues, consisting of 6,400 pages. It was the official publication of the Arizona State Teachers Association and included updates on educational research, feature stories, pleas for subscription checks, and even a regular "Hero Tales of Arizona" column by territorial historian Sharlot Hall.

Louise also wrote a column, "Editorial Comment," giving her recommendations for standardization of schools, a state fair, night schools, higher teacher salaries, and a state home for retired teachers.

In May 1918 Timothy Riordan, federal food administrator for Arizona, appointed Louise as state leader of college women. Her new responsibility was to initiate an organization among college women to carry out the food conservation program.

In 1919 there was no such thing as a national association for working women, although many women who worked felt the need for one, including Louise. She attended the first organizational meeting of the National Federation of Business and Professional Women, Inc. (BPW/USA) and realized the potential of this group to work for equal pay, opportunity, and education. She came home and founded a Business and Professional Women's Club in Yuma. Somehow, in spite of all her other responsibilities, she managed to visit all the other clubs—which meant driving 1,500 miles of gravel roads. It's just as well that one of her hobbies was motor trips!

In 1920 a cotton boom swept the country, driven in part by World War I. The War Department had ordered thousands of airplanes, all of which needed cotton fiber for their tires and for fabric to cover their wings. Cotton cultivation in Yuma exploded from eleven thousand acres in 1917 to twenty-seven thousand in 1920, while beef prices sank. In the Salt River Valley alone, thirty thousand of the fifty thousand dairy cattle were auctioned off.

That same year the Russell Sage Foundation conducted a comparative study and found that of the forty-eight states, Arizona had the third-best educational system in the nation, following Montana and California. Throughout the nation the lowest average salary for teachers was $25 per month in North Carolina, while the highest was $88 in California.

An article in the Arizona Daily Star jubilantly noted, "There are now 100 times as many pupils enrolled in high schools as there were in 1870. The number then was 19,000 and now it is nearly 2,000,000."

The writer then added that "the high school attendance has increased with great rapidity, but the new pupils have been mostly girls."

In 1920 Louise campaigned for a seat in the Arizona House of Representatives. The Yuma Morning Sun endorsed her candidacy:

When she takes her seat in the House of Representatives, which she will do as surely as the sun rises and sets, she will be one of the real leaders of the house. She is probably one of the best posted women in Arizona, and is regarded throughout the State as a real leader on all questions pertaining to the uplift of humanity, and especially as a champion of our public schools. She will go to Phoenix unhampered by domestic ties of any character. In a word, Miss Boehringer will be a great credit to Yuma County.

As predicted by the Yuma paper, she did win and served two one-year terms. While there, she served on the Counties and County Affairs Committee and was the chairman of the Committee on Education, where she presided over joint House and Senate education committee sessions.

Of the nine bills she introduced, one established the first per capita funding ($25 per schoolchild) for schools. Another created a state school board. But the one of which she was most proud was House Bill No. 170, which legitimized children born out of wedlock. The Delta Kappa Gamma Society wrote that "By virtue of this law, parents may be 'illegitimate,' but never the child."

In February 1921 she was elected the first state president of the National Federation of Business and Professional Women's Clubs. In August of that year, she began her second campaign for the state superintendent of schools job.

Arizona Republic wrote that, as representative, she had been "instrumental in having several bills passed which might be considered signal victories for the women of the state." The writer further noted:

Believing firmly that women should have a part in the political life of the country, Miss Boehringer has yet never taken the attitude that man is, as a whole, prejudiced to women holding office. During the ten years that she has been in office, she says that she has been well received by the men and that the only males who have ever denounced the Nineteenth amendment have been those who came from limited environment.

Louise lost in the primary, which infuriated one editorial writer in the Glendale newspaper. Under a headline of "Democrats Have Little Use for Women Officials," he seethed:

When democratic voters of Arizona nominated C. O. Case at the late primary for the office of State Superintendent of Public Instruction over Miss Boehringer, they put a premium on inefficiency in public office. . . . Miss Boehringer, who is known among school people of Arizona as one of the most capable and efficient school administrators in the state, backed up with a splendid record as county school superintendent of Yuma County and editor of The Arizona Teacher, went down with a decisive defeat by C. O. Case, whose record as former state superintendent has never set the world afire.

Actually, C. O. Case was a worthy adversary. He went on to become the longest tenured state superintendent in Arizona's history and is credited with improving rural school conditions, initiating night schools to teach English to non-native speakers, and establishing part-time instruction for working adolescent students.

In 1924 the annual convention of the Arizona Federation of Business and Professional Women's Clubs was held in Tucson, and Louise was again elected state president. In the April 12, 1924, edition of the

Tucson Citizen, she was reported as urging the organization to work toward banishing all illiteracy in the United States before 1930 and saying "that the percentage of illiteracy in Arizona was especially high and that therefore the work would be particularly hard."

Four years later, then-Secretary of Commerce Herbert Hoover appointed Louise as chair of the Arizona Better Homes in America Committee. Four thousand communities nationwide participated in the housing improvement program, and Pinal County—Louise was now based in Phoenix—was among the seventeen that won awards. Her responsibility was to adapt the national housing and home life improvement program to Arizona.

Never one to stagnate, Louise traveled to the University of California, Berkeley, four consecutive summers to take classes. In December 1930, at the age of fifty-two, she was awarded a master's degree in education. Her thesis was "Education and Experience Essential to Editorship of a State Educational Journal."

She also started both the Phoenix and Tucson branches of the National League of American Pen Women.

Toward the end of her time as a Berkeley student, she became more interested in the women who had gone before her, and she wrote biographies that were published in the Arizona Historical Review. They survive as a wonderful record of some of the state's most dynamic women, including then-octogenarian Mary Elizabeth Post, one of Arizona's pioneer teachers.

Three years later, in 1933, she was appointed director of curriculum for the state's Department of Education, a position she held for six years. She edited subject-matter courses and helped install the curricula throughout the state. During this time she was also named chairman of educational broadcasts.

Still not one to fritter away her vacation time, she also taught summer sessions at the Arizona State Teachers College in Flagstaff.

In 1939 she at last sold the Arizona Teacher to the Arizona Education Association. The magazine, and her position as editor, had long provided her with visibility and had served as a platform for her to express her views. In the September 1925 issue, she had welcomed teachers back to work by writing:

The September number will find the larger proportion of the teachers of the State back in their schoolrooms again. Another week will see them all at work. We wish to extend a personal greeting to every teacher in city, town or most remote schoolroom of our vast rural domain. Wherever you are, you are again facing an Opportunity. You are stimulating minds and developing characters—or you are not. The Opportunity is there. We are thinking especially of the young teacher today who enters the classroom of the public schools for the first time this September. Let no one cause your ideals to grow dim nor let any circumstance cause your ardor to grow less. There is no finer Opportunity in life than that of teaching boys and girls.

In 1940, at the age of sixty-two, Louise Boehringer announced her third run for superintendent of public instruction. According to the June 21 Arizona Daily Star, she said she "would continue to work for modern schools in Arizona, with the greatest benefit to the children of the state at the lowest possible cost to the taxpayers. She believes particularly in stressing the importance of American citizenship and American peace in the world of turmoil and war."

She lost the election and retired to live on her farm in Yuma.

In 1953 she moved to Seattle, where she lived quietly with her sister-in-law until she died on September 11, 1956.

Mary Kidder Rak

(1879–1958)
RANCHER AND WRITER

Mary sat against the adobe wall of the cabin, savoring the balmy November day and the solitude. Robles, a shepherd mix, lay at her feet, seeming to enjoy the peace as much as his mistress.

Mary's husband, Charlie, was away for ten days hauling steers to Los Angeles—an arduous trip from their twenty-two-thousand-acre ranch high in the Chiricahua Mountains of southeastern Arizona.

This wasn't the first time Charlie had left Mary alone at the ranch, and she always relished the respite. Except for thirty steers by the barn, all the horses and cattle were out on the range where browse was plentiful. Mary was happy for the unaccustomed hours of rest between morning and evening feeding.

"Basking in the sun, sometimes I sat and thought, sometimes I just sat," she wrote later in A Cowman's Wife.

And, besides, if any emergency did occur, she secretly considered herself completely capable of handling any situation that might arise.

The capricious weather of the Chiricahuas almost proved her wrong.

"Charlie, I am sure, would have recognized the unseasonably warm days for what they were, weather-breeders; but I was entirely unprepared for what was to come," she wrote.

The next morning, Mary awoke to a cloudy, oppressive day, and she used her time to fill the coal-oil lamps, gather wood for the fireplace and kitchen stove, and to bring in extra food from the storeroom. She always had a month's worth of supplies on hand because going to town was no easy jaunt for local ranchers in the 1930s. The nearest town was Douglas, five hours and fifty-six bone-jolting miles away.

Mary Kidder Rak Cochise County Historical Society

As an afterthought, she made one more trip to the barn and returned with a shovel.

In mid-afternoon, the temperature plummeted, and occasional flakes of snow wafted toward the dusty brown earth. Just in case of an approaching storm, she fed the steers an hour earlier than usual. By the time she'd finished, the wind was snatching the hay from the pitchfork, and she could "no longer see the near-by peaks, so thick was the falling snow. Falling is not quite the right term for it, either. Snow seemed to fill the air, coming from every direction at once. Even after it had reached the ground, whirling gusts seized upon the snow and bore it aloft, juggling the flakes in the air."

The chickens became so hysterical Mary had to catch and carry them, one by one, to the henhouse before retreating to the cabin with Robles.

All night the snow continued, and the wind howled as it uprooted trees, which then dragged the telephone line down as they fell.

When Mary rose the next morning, the storm had abated, but drifts jammed the doorways, and the thermometer revealed a most unusual temperature: five degrees below zero. She forced her way out the door and, grateful that she'd retrieved the shovel, she dug paths to the barn and then more paths to the feeding troughs for the cattle. No sooner had she wearily finished than the wind gathered strength again, and yet another snowstorm roared up the canyon.

By the third day the horses made their way down the mountain to the barn, hoping for grain because snow had buried all the grass, adding more mouths to feed. Again she shoveled out paths, again she fed the hungry livestock and chickens.

Five days after the storm, the paths around the ranch remained clear, but Mary "heard a sound that made my heart drop down into my rubber boots. Snow, melting on vast slopes, had reached the river, which now would roar down the canyon for days, fed from huge drifts on the high mountains above us." The road to Old Camp Rucker Ranch crossed the now-impassable White River five times. It would be days before anyone could drive in.

In the meantime Charlie had read the news about heavy snows in southern Arizona and had returned from California. He'd arranged to meet one of their neighbors in Douglas for a ride home, but the man didn't get far from his own ranch before becoming stuck in a snowdrift. Charlie was able to catch a ride to the southern end of the Chiricahua range, and then he walked four miles to another ranch, where he borrowed a horse and saddle.

Then, according to Mary, "he rode home through twelve miles of deep snow, over fallen logs and under snow-laden branches."

Her reaction to his unexpected appearance at the door?

"I wonder if real pioneer women ever cried for joy?"

❦

Mary Kidder Rak may not have considered herself a real pioneer woman, but she certainly worked as hard as any western settler. Like many other early 1900s ranch women, she was originally a city dweller and came to ranching late in life.

Pioneering, determination, and an itch to travel seem to have run in her family. Three of her ancestors came to America on the Mayflower, two were colonial governors, and five fought for the colonies in the American Revolution.

Mary's father, Ichabod Norton Kidder, was an attorney who was born in Edgartown, Massachusetts. In 1867, at the age of twenty-nine, his residence was listed as Boonesboro, Iowa, but when he married nineteen-year-old Eliza Allen Luce, it was in Tisbury, Massachusetts, on Martha's Vineyard. Twelve years later, Mary was born in Boone, Iowa, on August 4, 1879. No records have survived of Mary's childhood, but she apparently did spend some time on Martha's Vineyard with her mother's family.

In 1893 the Kidders moved to California, and Mary attended Troop Polytechnic Institute in Pasadena until 1896. According to one source, she aspired to a stage career but was persuaded by her family to attend college instead.

She attended Stanford University, and in 1901 she received a bachelor's degree in history. For several years she taught public school in San Francisco. From 1905 to 1917 she was a social worker in an organization called the Associated Charities, the first general, nonsectarian relief organization in the area (now the Family Service Agency of San Francisco).

In 1906 disaster struck the city. At 5:13 a.m., April 18, an earthquake shook the West from Coos Bay, Oregon, to Los Angeles, and east to central Nevada. Fires blazed throughout San Francisco for four days straight, and vast tenements collapsed as the ground melted beneath their foundations. Three thousand people died, and the damage was estimated at $500 million.

The Associated Charities directed earthquake relief for the city, and the following year it established an employment bureau to help during the economic depression brought on by the earthquake and fire.

During the next few years, the group also set up a Department of Unmarried Mothers and Their Babies, which allowed the closing of "foundling asylums" and led to improved foster care and adoption programs. Sometime during this period, Mary became superintendent of the Associated Charities.

Like Mary Kidder, Charles Lukeman Rak, a cowpuncher from New Mexico and Texas, had also moved to California. The two met while he was in school at Berkeley studying forestry. They were married March 30, 1917, and soon moved to Tucson, where Mary taught at the University of Arizona, and Charlie worked for the state forest service.

It wasn't long before she put her social service experience to work. In 1919 she sent questionnaires covering forty-eight topics, including "The Care of the Feeble-minded," child welfare, use of school buildings for recreational and social purposes, county jails, and "Homes for Aged and Infirm Arizona Pioneers," to every philanthropic and service agency in the state.

Based on the responses, she compiled A Social Survey of Arizona. In the introduction she wrote as follows: "It is earnestly hoped that the splendid flood of social service enthusiasm, which had its source in devoted war work, will be diverted into peace channels and find some guidance in this little Survey." She was unafraid to express her own opinion:

A county jail is an unpleasant place which we would all prefer comfortably to ignore, but since its unwilling inmates will sooner or later be free to mingle with their fellows on the outside, it is of the greatest importance to all of us that they come forth in better physical, mental and more condition than when their imprisonment began.

It is earnestly hoped that those who read this bulletin will be willing to go to their county jail—for an hour—and see its conditions. So long as no one enters a jail except under compulsion,

*there is very little likelihood of improvement, which must be pre-
ceded by public interest.*

Mary and Charlie never had children of their own, but she was obviously concerned about youngsters. As she expressed it in the survey:

*Arizona children are very fortunate in their wonderful climate
which makes an outdoor life possible all the year, and in their
almost limitless room for play. However, it is to be remembered
that every community in the United States was once small
enough to afford open space for its children's development, and
many of these communities found out later that their rapid
growth had wiped out the vacant lot play-space, and that it had
to be replaced at great expense. . . . The women of each community could do nothing more useful than interesting themselves
in the lives and problems of the children who come before the
juvenile court.*

That same year, when Mary was forty, the couple grew tired of city
life and bought the Old Camp Rucker Ranch deep in the Chiricahua
Mountains. The ranch house was the old adobe fort used in the cam-
paigns against Geronimo's Apaches in the 1880s. It was nestled among
junipers and surrounded by rocky peaks, some close to ten thousand
feet. Several years later, the fort burned, forcing the Raks to move to a
bunkhouse so small that Charlie said one "couldn't cuss the cat without
getting fur in your mouth."

Although at first she knew nothing about cattle ("Moreover, I was
terrified when the mildest cow even looked my way"), Mary watched
and learned. Within a few years she was as competent at managing the
livestock as Charlie, and even had her own brand because their second
ranch was in her name.

Not all men regarded business-savvy females as favorably as her husband. Like most women in cow country during those days, when someone came by to talk ranching, Mary retreated to the background and left the men to their conversation. But often Charlie was away for long periods, leaving her to run the enterprise. Occasionally, she needed to transact a sale or business deal—provided "the man would allow me to do so."

Sometimes, after handling some unimportant business matter with a man during Charlie's temporary absence, I go to the mirror and scan my countenance anxiously, wondering if I really look as foolish and incompetent as these men seem to think me. On the ranch is an unfortunate cow who has been named Ballasa, because of a bullet which a careless hunter once sent through her lower jaw. Her mouth is always hanging open; she drools; she looks almost as foolish as the deer-hunter who shot her. After an encounter with some man who assumes that I am incapable of the simplest business transaction, I even fancy I must resemble that poor cow.

Mary spent many hours on horseback, searching for unbranded calves or retrieving heifers for extra feeding. She helped brand, medicate, and vaccinate the cows, and was out almost daily searching for broken fences, monitoring wolf traps, separating out animals bound for sale, checking watering spots, or performing any other of the myriad tasks required by ranchers. Working cattle involves much more than sitting on a well-trained horse. As she once described it: "After a day riding up and down our rocky mountainsides and through oak thickets after cattle, I am convinced the cattle are really working us."

Yet, as tiring as the outside work was, Mary never minded. She loved the sunsets, the sudden downpours, the vaqueros, the spectacular mountain pinnacles surrounding the Rucker basin, and the company of horses and dogs.

"It is not all 'beer and skittles' anywhere," she wrote her New York City friend Gertrude Hills in August 1934, "but I would rather take my hardships in the open. And I know, for I spent three years in a schoolroom and eleven in an office before coming here."

On top of her outdoor chores, Mary's responsibilities also included baking bread, churning butter, putting up preserves, and cooking meals for however many visitors and hired hands were at the ranch that week. Although it was far from her favorite task, she also cleaned the house, giving it "a lick and a promise"—no easy job in a dusty climate without modern conveniences.

However, what's most remarkable about Mary Rak is not her achievement as a ranch woman, but as a writer. Somehow, between keeping house and riding the range, she found time to maintain a lively correspondence—and to write several books and a couple of plays. Each week she resolved to write a thousand words, but finding the time was always a challenge. Many a woman writer can share these sentiments:

> *Really my chief problem is to get time to write. I am so infernally bogged down by housekeeping and other jobs and never, never can I count absolutely upon an uninterrupted hour. I cook, clean, wash, mend,—do housekeeping without many conveniences—boss the men when Charlie is away and there is no one to see that I have any time free from interruptions. . . . There is a cave up the canyon. Sometime I'll evict the mountain lioness and her cubs and move in. Her reputation will serve me well.*

Mary's first book, A Social Survey of Arizona, came out in 1921. A Cowman's Wife and Mountain Cattle were collections of essays about ranch life and were published in 1934 and 1936 by Houghton Mifflin, and fifteen thousand words of the latter appeared in Cosmopolitan magazine in 1936.

"My endeavor is to write of our own day in a manner that will interest our contemporaries, and at the same time so truthfully that the books may have an historical value if they survive," she told the Arizona Daily Star in 1938.

That same year Border Patrol was published, and They Guard the Gates appeared in 1941. By then, Mary felt she'd used up the ranch material and was ready for something different. She wrote in a September 21, 1941, letter to her friend, Bobbie Scott:

> *I am recovering from having written a book. The worst stage of the whole business is waiting anywhere from one month to three for a report from a publisher. If the first one decides it is no good then I'll send it off again and wait another spell. Just because I had to have a change and saw no other way to get it, I wrote a mystery. It was hot and dry and whenever I felt mad I hauled off and shot one of my characters. Just barely had left enough to wind up the book, all villains being killed or on their way to jail by chapter 31. If I ever write another, I shall start with more characters so I can kill more and not peter out.*

In April 1936 Charlie came down with a combination of flu, pneumonia, and jaundice. He refused to go to the hospital and then became too ill to be moved into town. That same year, Mary was felled by the flu three times in several months. By that time the Raks owned two ranches, Old Camp Rucker in the Chiricahuas and a smaller ranch, Hell's Hip Pocket Ranch, thirty miles away.

Much as they loved the Rucker ranch, the couple reluctantly resolved to sell it. Two ranches thirty miles apart were too much work and too much duplication of effort. The war intervened, but finally Mrs. W. S. (Ella) Dana of New York City bought the property in 1943. She was a wealthy woman who owned another ranch in Nevada, in addition to her Long Island residence.

Mary seems to have had mixed feelings about the sale. Although she was relieved, she described Mrs. Dana as someone "who needs a ranch no more than a cat needs a fig." (Mrs. Dana turned the ranch over to the USDA Forest Service in 1970.)

Moving and getting settled into the smaller ranch took longer than Mary had anticipated. She sounded discouraged in a letter to Gertrude Hills: "Of course I am not writing at present, and that is small loss to anyone since I have three unsold books on hand, which I do not expect to sell during the war, if ever."

Six years later, in 1949, a stroke left Mary unable to write. She died in a Douglas hospital on January 25, 1958, and her ashes were scattered over her ranch.

Thirteen days later, Charlie died. But Mary and her husband live on: The entire Rak estate was left to the University of Arizona for the Mary Kidder Rak scholarship fund for students in agriculture and home economics. All of her papers, including the original manuscripts of the unpublished Mystery at Pecos High Bridge, The Dark Brown Mystery, and At the Crossroads of Life are still available for perusal at the Special Collections section of the University of Arizona library.

Most of all, her ranch books are a legacy that continues to show how one woman took on life in the West and made it her own. A literary friend of the family wrote after Mary's death: "Of all the books which attempt to tell about life on a modern cattle ranch, these two [A Cowman's Wife and Mountain Cattle] seem to me to be the truest and the best."

Mary-Russell Ferrell Colton

(1889–1971)

PAINTER OF SOUTHWESTERN LIGHT

*As I walked up the lane in the last golden glow a coyote called
from Switzer's Mesa & presently a whole chorus joined in from
somewhere up back of Dry Lake Mountain. I stood and listened
to the voices of the wild and thrilled beneath those wondrous
peaks, and presently as I looked, they changed to rose, glowing
like dream mountains in the land that never was, then slowly
they grew cold and so very, very awesome and I hurried home to
the warmth of our little shack.*

Mary-Russell Colton, who wrote those stirring words, and her
young son, Ferrell, would be alone in the shack for another month.

It was the summer of 1916, and polio had hit Philadelphia, where
Mary-Russell, her husband, Harold, and their son, Ferrell, lived during the school year. The Coltons loved the Southwest and spent every
summer exploring and camping, usually in the pine-covered mountains
around Flagstaff. Trained as a painter, Mary-Russell especially savored
the clear light and saturated colors of the northern Arizona landscape.

After reading newspaper accounts of the epidemic back East, the
couple decided Harold would return alone to resume teaching, leaving
Mary-Russell and Ferrell safely in Arizona until late fall.

In one sense the separation was difficult because Mary-Russell had
not been apart from Harold since the start of their marriage. But the
transplanted Easterner also relished the chance to work and explore on
her own. Her letters to Harold described her painting "fever" and how
the surrounding peaks inspired her.

Mary-Russell Ferrell Colton Museum of Northern Arizona

The extended stay also gave her more opportunity to search for Indian ruins. The day before she was scheduled to return to Pennsylvania, Mary-Russell rode out alone.

[R]ode up past the Greenlaw mill and struck indirectly toward Elden. . . . Crossing the lumber railroad I soon came out upon a very high mound, and suddenly realized that I had found the largest Pueblo we have yet come upon. I should say it had been quite equal in size to Walpi, the buildings at the northern end having been at least 2 story, & I believe 3 story, the entire mound is over 15 feet high. . . . Tomorrow I return to make measurements & a sketch & collect pottery for you. I was quite thrilled over my find.

Mary-Russell had every reason to be thrilled. Even today, Elden Pueblo is still studied by archaeologists and plays "a groundbreaking role in making archaeology and the history of Arizona's earliest residents more accessible to the public."

∽

Mary-Russell Ferrell didn't come from a family of painters or archaeologists. Her father, Joseph, was an engineer, descended from a long line of Pennsylvania farmers. Her mother, Elise Houston, was from the noted Polk family of Tennessee.

Mary-Russell was born at her grandparents' Louisville, Kentucky, home on March 25, 1889, and was named for her aunt, Mary-Russell Buchanan. Her sister, Griselda, was four years older, but she died from diphtheria when Mary-Russell was two.

Her early childhood was a happy one. Joseph Ferrell developed Broadwater Island, a resort for well-to-do Philadelphians. The family spent summers there in what Mary-Russell later called "my childhood paradise," and she fished, hiked, and roamed the island, trailing a retinue of dogs, lambs, geese, chickens, and a Chincoteague pony. She was a quiet child who preferred solitude, reading, and sketching.

She attended Pelham Academy. Much later, she wrote that her "formal" education was "most casual by today's standards" because she learned mathematics from her father, history from her mother, and composition from her aunt. She left Pelham before graduation.

By 1904 Mary-Russell knew she wanted to be an artist and to travel. She was ready to start academic art training, but in July her father died, leaving the family in uncertain financial condition. Elise Ferrell was forced to sell the Broadwater cottage, and mother and daughter moved to a local boardinghouse.

In November, Mary-Russell was accepted at the prestigious Philadelphia School of Design for Women, and, fortunately, a family friend paid her tuition.

There she learned to clean and restore old paintings, and she made friends who were to remain a part of her life for the next forty years. Although she was described as strikingly beautiful, she lived a chaste and diligent life—no dating, no makeup, and at five feet two inches, she even refused to wear high heels.

In 1908 her mother married Theodore Presser, owner of Presser Music Publishing House. The marriage eased Elise's monetary worries, but Mary-Russell, who still lived at home, clashed with her new stepfather. The following summer, Elise suggested Mary-Russell travel to the Selkirk Mountains of British Columbia with Dr. Charles Shaw, a botanist who often took students on his expeditions.

Mary-Russell reveled in the experience. She sketched, camped, rode horses, and hiked in—gasp!—bloomers. She broke a rib in a sledding accident but reassured her mother she was having a wonderful time and was "a new woman living a new life."

The following summer Dr. Shaw asked her to return, and he also invited Harold S. Colton, a young zoology instructor at the University of Pennsylvania. This second trip was grueling and perhaps overly ambitious. Tragically, Shaw was killed in a river accident. The subdued students returned east slowly, passing through Arizona and New Mexico.

The physical and emotional challenges of the trip forced Mary-Russell to examine herself and the life she'd led. In a letter to her stepfather, she asked for his friendship and added:

> *The wilderness of which you have such a horror holds no terrors for me, no, not even now. It beckons, beckons and claims its own, that is all, and if it is God's will, I will go back again, sometime but not next year. But the city and the places that are old with man shall never hold me. I must breathe.*

That summer of 1910 witnessed the flowering of Mary-Russell's love for the American Southwest—as well as for young Harold. They were engaged the following spring, which marked the end of her own financial concerns. Harold had several trust funds and was able to teach without being paid to do so.

The couple was married May 23, 1912, and spent their honeymoon in Pecos, New Mexico. Mary-Russell wrote her mother from there:

> *[We] get along real well, considering we've been married almost two weeks. We ride and hike over the mesas and along the roaring Pecos, and paint and read and sleep and eat and are both perfectly fine. I have 6 sketches already, it is a great country to paint in.*

On that same trip they visited Flagstaff, little knowing it would later become home, and spent the whole summer camping throughout the West. They also bought two old Hopi blankets, a small start of what would become the Museum of Northern Arizona collection.

The following summer, they again migrated to the Southwest, where they hiked in the Sangre de Cristo Mountains, with two pack burros and a wagon, then visited the Taos, San Juan, and Santa Clara Pueblos, among others.

Mary-Russell loved it all and wrote her mother:

Riding for a month caused me to lose flesh, & when I return you will be surprised to find you have a hipless daughter. . . . But don't think that I am fading away from ill health for I am solid muscle from head to toe & have been enjoying good health all summer. I can be in the saddle from dawn to dark, ride forty-five miles a day, without feeling tired, so you see dear, I am not an ill woman, in spite of the hipless condition.

She must have been healthy indeed, for on August 30, 1914, she gave birth to a sturdy baby boy, Joseph Ferrell Colton.

In 1916 the young family rented a ranch in Flagstaff for the summer. Little Ferrell set his parents on a new course when he showed them a potsherd he'd found. Mary-Russell and Harold were so intrigued they traveled to the Museum of the Southwest in Los Angeles to learn more about prehistory. From then on they resolved to map, record, and protect the ruins around Flagstaff, and they were the first to conduct an archaeological study in the area. It was later that summer that Mary-Russell discovered the Elden Pueblo.

In spite of marriage, motherhood, and her new fascination with archaeology, Mary-Russell had not stopped painting. Early in 1917 she and some classmates formed "The Ten Philadelphia Women Painters," later called "The Philadelphia Ten" when sculptors were admitted. The group continued to hold annual exhibits and traveling shows until 1945.

On September 4, 1917, Mary-Russell gave birth to Sabin Woolworth Colton IV. The delivery was difficult, and, according to one biographer, "This birth seems to have disturbed her equilibrium, and for the rest of her life, she suffered one complaint after another as well as a persistent nervous disorder."

By now America was several months into World War I, and Harold was working for the U.S. Army in Washington, D.C. Mary-Russell was ill with the flu, the baby with "milk sickness," and Ferrell with pneumonia. Gradually, her mother nursed everyone back to health, and by June the family was able to return to Flagstaff.

During the summer of 1921, some of Mary-Russell's energy returned, thanks to a partial hysterectomy that treated the infected wounds remaining from Sabin's birth four years earlier. She worked hard at her easel and exhibited five new paintings. But most significantly that year, Mary-Russell and Harold met Jesse C. Clarke, a local postal worker and self-educated archaeologist. During the many hours and meals shared by the threesome, the idea of a Flagstaff museum was born.

The following year, Mary-Russell's mother, Elise, left her husband, Ted Presser, and came to live with the Coltons. She died on November 7, 1922, from complications from a bleeding gastric ulcer. Mary-Russell was so devastated that Harold took a sabbatical so the family could flee the East to spend the winter in Tucson.

With spring came temperatures near the century mark, and the family escaped to northern Arizona. They collected more Hopi crafts—all the while wondering why six-year-old Sabin was so pale and lethargic. He was diagnosed with valley fever, and in spite of all medical help, he died May 4, 1924. Mary-Russell was never the same after his death.

Thanks to Harold's financial portfolio and Mary-Russell's inheritance, the Coltons were wealthy. They sold their Pennsylvania home, with all its sad memories, and in 1926 settled in a house they built on the Flagstaff land where they'd camped so many summers.

In spite of her grief, Mary-Russell sent four new paintings to the annual Philadelphia Ten show. One won first prize and the following review: "In the work of Mrs. Colton, one feels an underlying sense of the grandeur of nature and the inconsequence of man."

During the next few years, the couple continued to buy land and develop their collection of relics and archaeological studies.

In May 1928 the first board of trustees of the Northern Arizona Society of Science and Art appointed Harold as president and Mary-Russell as both curator of art and organizer of the arts and crafts section. The Coltons donated their extensive collection of artifacts, and Mary-Russell, seeing a decline in Hopi arts and crafts, initiated a new exhibition to revive their style.

In 1929 the family gave $2,500—more than $20,000 in today's currency—to what had become the Museum of Northern Arizona.

A year later Mary-Russell inaugurated the Exhibition of Arizona Artists, which included three of her own works, and also sponsored a show of art by Native American children of Tuba City schools. In addition she sent eleven paintings to traveling Ten shows.

January 1930 marked the beginning of the decade that was to be the peak of Mary-Russell's life. She found new energy and completed thirty-four paintings. In addition she decided her next mission would be to revive Hopi arts and crafts, particularly textiles, pottery, and silversmithing.

That spring, somewhat nervously, she set the wheels in motion for the first Hopi Craftsman Exhibition. The Coltons visited all twelve Hopi pueblos and gathered two truckloads of entries.

A thousand people attended, and on July 2, 1930, Harold described the inaugural event:

Indians swarmed in from the Reservation. The Assistant Commissioner of Indian Affairs dropped in from Washington. Then the dry season broke with a gentle rain, which was interpreted to mean that the benevolent Kachinas that dwell in the towering Peaks above the town, were pleased. It was, therefore, a huge success.

Making a technical improvement in her own work, Mary-Russell discovered that an underlay of gesso gave a brilliance to her paintings that was much more representative of the Southwestern light. She also began studying Hopi dyes and set up a minilab in her studio, performing such experiments as boiling various weeds in sheep urine.

For someone plagued with both physical and emotional difficulties, Mary-Russell had phenomenal drive and energy. In May 1931 she added a Junior Art Show to the other exhibitions she sponsored. It was her belief that

> *Art education must begin with children. We must grow our own artists. The material is here awaiting encouragement and cultivation. All about us is great beauty, grandeur of form, glory of color, sweep of opalescent desert, dark forests and snow capped peaks. Nowhere in the world has man a more beautiful setting. Children are sensitive to color and beauty. Young Arizona is growing up with a remarkable background and a great opportunity.*

By 1932 Mary-Russell was knowledgeable enough about Hopi folklore that the Bureau of Indian Affairs often consulted her, and in 1933 the museum board appointed her curator of ethnology, as well as curator of art.

The 1930s saw more donations to the museum from the Coltons, including twenty-nine acres in memory of Sabin. But probably Mary-Russell's most significant contribution was the influence of her artist's eye. At the time Hopi silver work was an imitation of Navajo design. Mary-Russell's idea was to transfer the tribe's own symbols from their pottery and basketry to their silver, and Virgil Hubert, the assistant art director of the museum, suggested an overlay technique. Mary-Russell then contacted all the Hopi silversmiths, saying she'd buy anything that incorporated the new design. After a slow start, the Hopi Silver Project took off and made the tribe's style what it is today.

In 1940 Mary-Russell turned fifty, and both her health and energy dwindled.

The December 7, 1941, attack on Pearl Harbor was a tremendous blow and one that she took personally. She lost interest in painting and, for the first time in her life, had her waist-length hair cut short. She devoted all her time to her victory garden and her work as chair of the Red Cross's Nurse's Aide program.

Although the museum flourished after the war, Mary-Russell did not. By 1950 her vacillating emotions and personality changes dominated the family's life. Although her physicians blamed "atherosclerosis of the brain," modern doctors would have diagnosed Alzheimer's disease.

In 1951 she painted for the last time, although she still enjoyed doing pencil drawings and charcoal portraits.

By 1958 Mary-Russell's irascibility had driven off the servants, and Harold resigned his position as museum director to take care of her and attempt to finish his own projects. A year later, she'd grown increasingly paranoid and, feeling slighted one day, even withdrew her museum membership.

Fortunately, she was able to enjoy one last bright spot of recognition. In 1959 the Indian Arts and Crafts Board of the United States Department of the Interior awarded her a Citation of Merit, which read, in part, as follows:

> *You came from the East into a land which was new and strange to you. Soon you found a new life into which you fit yourself so naturally that you have become as one. Quietly you approached the Indian artist with the warmth of a friend and the humility of a learner, and he responded by giving generously of his culture. To this you added a depth of perception and artistic sensitivity which enabled you to measure his strengths and limitations.*

Realizing that this was expressive of a great tradition and part of our national heritage, you exercised every effort to perpetuate this tradition so that generations yet to come might also enjoy it. . . .

Rarely does a non-Indian have the opportunity to establish an Indian tradition. Yet, in 1938, you proposed a development in Hopi silversmithing which had a long, slow genesis. Today that style of silverwork has become familiar, and is popularly regarded as representing a traditional craft expression of these people. But you were careful not to dictate; yours was the role of counselor—in truth, a pupil turned teacher.

By 1962 Mary-Russell was no longer the person she had been, nor even a reasonable adult. Harold, now in his early eighties and already ill with the strain of caring for her, was felled by a stroke. The poor man had difficulty recuperating because Mary-Russell tried to punch any nurse who dared enter his bedroom.

Finally on August 12, 1962, Mary-Russell attacked Harold with a paperweight. Her distraught husband had her sedated and taken to Camelback Hospital in Phoenix in the only vehicle available on a Sunday afternoon: the mortician's ambulance.

She never returned home. Three days later, Harold had another stroke.

Christmas 1962 was the first Christmas in fifty years that Harold and Mary-Russell spent apart. By now she had forgotten every detail of her life except for a few childhood memories of the Broadwater cottage. The family arranged to move her to a nursing home, where she spent her remaining nine years.

On December 29, 1970, at the age of eighty-nine, Harold Colton died. Ferrell, now living in Flagstaff with his wife and children, took his father's ashes to the family plot in Philadelphia.

Seven months later, on July 16, 1971, Mary-Russell Ferrell Colton died at age eighty-two.

Much earlier, she had asked that the ashes "of my husband may be mingled with mine, when they both shall be committed to the winds of heaven. It is desired that the ashes be released from a plane over the cedar country, on the Painted Desert, east of the Peaks."

For whatever reason, Harold and Mary-Russell's ashes remain buried side by side in the Colton family plot just outside Philadelphia.

CARMEN LEE BAN

(1891–1940)

CULTURAL PIONEER

The six girls—five Lee sisters and their friend Rita—had all been chattering so happily that the winter afternoon had turned into evening without anyone noticing.

"Please," said their hostess, "Won't you stay for dinner? We have plenty." Aurelia, Concepción, Maria Louisa, and Mariana all exchanged quick glances. They looked to Carmen, the oldest.

She smiled. "We'd love to," she said.

A little while later, they all gathered around the table, where a large bowl of soup, rich with meat and vegetables, awaited them. Each person had a flat ceramic spoon, and in the place of forks and knives, the sisters found chopsticks.

Muffled giggles moved around the table as pieces of meat and chunks of bok choy found new life, escaping back into bowls and skidding across plates.

"It was really embarrassing!" Mariana told her mother indignantly when they all returned home to Nogales that night. "The people kept saying, 'You're Chinese, and you don't know how to use chopsticks? You might as well not be Chinese!' They had to give us forks to eat with."

"It's true," Carmen said quietly. "I was ashamed to be Chinese and not do things Chinese people do."

Lai Ngan looked at her dispirited daughters. She said, "Hereafter you are going to learn to eat with chopsticks. Tomorrow, we buy what we need—and I'll give you lessons in Chinese eating."

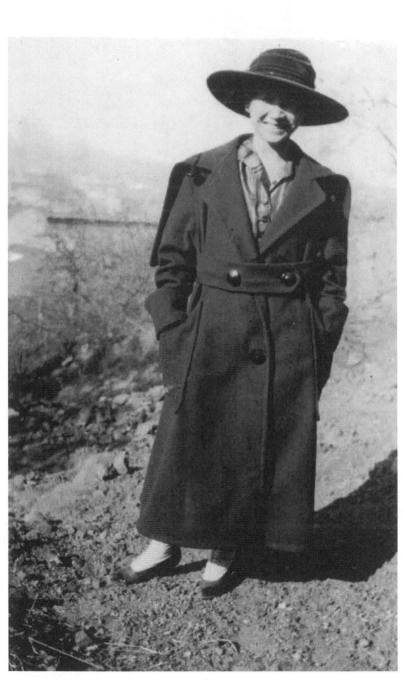

Carmen Lee Ban Arizona Historical Society, Tucson, AHS PC202F.4/D

The story of the Chinese experience in Arizona is one of long hours, hard work, and frugal living. Surprisingly, perhaps, it's also a tale of three nations, not two. Few families illustrate this aspect of Arizona history as well as that of Carmen Lee Ban.

Discouraged by the political and economic turmoil in the wake of the Opium Wars, the Taiping Rebellion, the Sino-Japanese war, and the Boxer Rebellion, 2.5 million people left China between 1840 and 1900. Those who came to America arrived in California, many lured by the hope of gold, others by work on the railroads. Some, like Carmen's grandparents, remained in San Francisco only a short time. They were actors in a Chinese opera company that toured in the 1870s, and when they returned to China with the opera, they left Carmen's mother, Lai Ngan, in the care of relatives.

Others stayed in the country and kept heading east; the first officially documented Chinese in Arizona were twenty men working in the Vulture Mine near Wickenburg in 1868. The first Chinese woman was recorded in Prescott in 1871; her name is lost, and all that's known is that she came with her husband. We also know that the first Chinese laundry opened in Phoenix in 1872. But it was the Southern Pacific Railroad that eventually drew huge numbers of Asians to Arizona.

By 1882 more than three hundred thousand Chinese had come to work in America, and even as early as 1877, nearly six hundred were in Yuma alone. In 1880 the first train pulled into Tucson, and the census listed 1,630 Chinese in Arizona not until 1950 would the state see that many Chinese residents again.

And they certainly did work: Chinese laborers laid nearly a mile of track a day from Yuma to Casa Grande, much of it in blistering heat. They were paid $1 a day (50 cents less than their white counterparts), from which they were expected to pay their own board.

Ironically, it was that hard work of the Chinese that made them a target of resentment. From the very beginning the new arrivals ran into prejudice and racism. In 1852 California levied a tax on foreign miners, and during the economic slump of the 1870s, the first shouts of "yellow peril!" began to be heard across the country. By 1883 one out of every four miners in Clifton was Chinese, until anti-Asian prejudice drove them out of the mines and into the jobs that no one else wanted and the service industries. Then, they found opportunities in almost every town, according to the Arizona State Historic Preservation Office:

> [I]t was a rare Arizona settlement that did not have a Chinese launderer, cook, or produce farmer, or all three, in the late nineteenth century. The energetic sojourners set up laundries, restaurants, and groceries in mining camps, construction camps, farming communities, Indian reservations, and towns. Anywhere there were customers for their services. In telling the story of Chinese in Arizona, the question is not "Where were they?" but "Where weren't they?"

Although Arizona didn't see the violence and race riots that occurred elsewhere in the West, being on the receiving end of rampant xenophobia was still a part of Chinese life in America. In Bisbee a rule that stood until the early 1930s prohibited Chinese from spending a night in town. In 1879 the Arizona Daily Miner announced that "Prescott has about 75 or 80 Chinamen, which is 75 or 80 too many. Now is a good time to get rid of them."

Similar attitudes throughout the nation culminated in the Chinese Exclusion Act of 1882, which prohibited immigration of Chinese workers for ten years. Only educated individuals and their families, or those born in this country, were allowed to immigrate. Anyone leaving the country had to register, and the new law forced all Chinese to carry a certificate of residence with a photograph—a requirement that would later provide employment for young Carmen Lee.

A decade later, in 1893, the act was renewed with even more stringent restrictions.

It wasn't long before the Chinese perceived Mexico as much friendlier territory than the United States. Even as early as 1873, two Chinese shoe and clothing factories prospered in Guaymas. From 1890 on, the Chinese in the northernmost state of Sonora had the biggest immigrant population. One way around the exclusion acts, especially for the Arizona Chinese, was to come in through Mexico, either illegally or as Mexican residents.

These were the times into which Carmen Lee was born on September 3, 1891, at her parents' house on Stockton Street in San Francisco. At age fifteen, Carmen's mother Lai Ngan had wed Lee Kwong, a gambling man and one whose family, like hers, had been part of the opera world. It was an arranged marriage.

Lee Kwong and Lai Ngan's first child was Percy Yeung Lee, born around 1889. Carmen arrived two years later, and her younger sister, Aurelia, was born around 1893.

Somewhat confusingly, Carmen was also known as Lee Cun, Le Cum (according to her mother), and, later, as Mrs. Ng Ban Sing, although she eventually dropped the "Ng."

Perhaps one reason the Chinese experience in Arizona hasn't been well documented is the difficulty English-speaking writers have with the Chinese language and naming conventions. Often, the Chinese characters have several pronunciations depending on dialect, and they're translated into English in various ways. For example, many of the nineteenth-century immigrants came from the southeastern Chinese province near Hong Kong known in English as "Kwangtung," "Guangdong," or "Canton."

To confuse the issue still more, many of the Chinese immigrants who entered illegally abandoned their given names to take on those of already established citizens. Ban Sing wasn't the real name of the man who would become Carmen's husband; his name was actually Lim Yuen Cong.

When the child known as Carmen was around two years old, Lee Kwong received a letter from friends in Mexico, asking for his help to look for gold. So, he packed his belongings and those of little four-year-old Percy and left Lai Ngan with the two girls.

Nearly a century later, Ngan is still remembered by her grandson as a fiercely determined and enterprising woman. ("She rolled her own cigarettes," Edward Ban said, chuckling. "None of us kids could do that!") She grew tired of waiting to hear from her husband, packed the family belongings, gathered up Carmen and Aurelia, and traveled to Mexico by steamer to find her husband.

The trip must have been grueling for the young mother: Anti-Asian sentiment was running strong, and, according to Mike Tom, Carmen's cousin and Ngan's grandchild by her second marriage, U.S. Customs officials on the steamer confiscated the family's registration certificates. More than twenty years later, Lai Ngan, Carmen, and Percy would all have to testify to the inspector in charge at the Immigration Service in Nogales to apply for citizenship in the very country where the children had been born.

Amazingly, Carmen's mother was able to find Lee Kwong, who was working a gold mine at La Colorada, southeast of Hermosillo.

Mexico was still a more comfortable place for the Chinese than the United States. Prejudice in America was growing, and in fact a 1901 Arizona law made marriage between the Chinese and Anglos a crime, stating "the marriage of a person of Caucasian blood with a Negro or Mongolian is null and void." The 1900 census only shows thirty-two Chinese women in Arizona, while the 1903 census shows three thousand Chinese living in Sonora. Hermosillo and Guaymas were both commercially important for Arizona, and at least ten of the thirty-seven Sonoran shoe factories were owned by Chinese.

One of those factories was where Lai Ngan found her first job. Lee Kwong continued mining. One photograph shows him with eight other men outside La Colorada Mine, all holding rifles, ready for the all-too-frequent Indian raids. Incongruously, his other hand is holding that of his young son, Percy, who in turn is holding firmly onto Carmen, then just a toddler.

Later, Lai Ngan opened a boardinghouse and ran her own small grocery store near the La Colorada Mine. She worked hard enough that she was able to save enough money to buy a small house, but at some point her husband lost it gambling. In a 1979 interview, Carmen's younger sister, Mariana, remembered:

One day a man came over and said to her, "You owe me some rent." She said, "What do you mean I owe you some rent? I bought this house myself." My mother got so mad. She got a stick and told him, "You get out of here and don't you ever come back looking for rent because I'm not going to give it to you. This is my house and I don't care how many times he sold it, it's mine." So the man never came back. When we left La Colorada, my mother just left the house and never got any money for it; maybe my father did.

During this time Carmen attended public elementary school in Guaymas, and Lai Ngan had five more children: Concepción, Maria Louisa, Mariana, Teresa, and Frank.

By 1905, when Carmen was fourteen, Lai Ngan moved the family north to the border town of Nogales, still in the Mexican state of Sonora.

Two months later, they moved again, this time to the Arizona side of Nogales, where they were the first Chinese family to settle. There, they lived behind the Morley Street grocery store, run by Lai Ngan. Lee Kwong followed a little later and worked selling lottery tickets. Eventually, they moved to an adobe brick house on the hill behind the city hall.

Carmen spent her school years in the Santa Cruz County school system and her out-of-school hours helping her mother in the store. By now she was fluent in both Spanish and English, but spoke only a few words of Chinese. Her son Edward remembers that although the immediate family always spoke English at home, his mother and aunts all spoke Spanish among themselves.

The massive destruction of the San Francisco earthquake in April of 1906 brought one benefit to the Chinese community, including the Lee family. Most of the records of those already in this country were destroyed; there was no longer evidence of where Lai Ngan or Lee Kwong had been born.

The 1910 census shows ten Chinese women in Phoenix, all of whom were married with children. In that same year the Mexican Revolution began, and the thirty-five thousand Chinese who lived there suddenly found themselves unwelcome.

In 1911 Sun Yat-Sen established a republic and overthrew the imperial Manchurian government. Even the Chinese who'd settled far away were affected. Women stopped binding their feet, and men stopped wearing their hair in the long braid down their backs that had shown their loyalty to the old regime.

By 1914 Percy had moved back to San Francisco, where he worked for an import-export company. Lee Kwong, who still missed the city of his early immigration years, went to visit his son and unfortunately had a stroke and died during the trip.

By the First World War, American attitudes toward the Chinese, though not "enlightened," were beginning to soften. One 1918 writer pointed out that the seventy thousand "Chinese in America are more than good laundry men and unsurpassed cooks," and that they were

> *honest, hard-working people. They have all the attributes that citizens of a democracy should have. As the prejudice which Americans formerly felt against their yellowskinned neighbors wears off, Americans are appreciating the absolute integrity and faithfulness of these people. Young mothers feel safe in trusting the baby to the family Chinaman; families will leave jewelry or money about, if the servants in the house are Chinese. They have the most extraordinary reputation of honesty of any race.*

Perhaps this grudging recognition was part of what convinced Carmen and her family to apply for what was known as a "return certificate" as a native. In 1917, she, Percy, and Lai Ngan were all interviewed by the United States Immigration Service, and each testified on behalf of the others that they had indeed moved from San Francisco to Mexico and then to Nogales, Arizona.

It was also at about this time that Carmen needed an extra job to help support the family. She chose photography and began to work behind the camera as well as doing the developing, printing, and retouching at Newman Photographer's in Nogales. When the business was sold in 1918 and became Albert W. Lohn, Photographer, Carmen continued to work there.

In 1919 Carmen and her younger sister Louise moved to Miami, Arizona, just east of Phoenix, where they were able to use their photographic experience working for Kelley Studios. A young man named Ban Sing had become acquainted with Carmen in Nogales and must have been quite enamored, for he made the hundred-mile trip to Miami several times to visit her.

On October 18, 1919, Carmen and Ban Sing were married, and Carmen moved to Tucson, where she would spend the rest of her life. Lai Ngan must have been pleased with her daughter's choice, for Ban Sing was a hard worker. On the rare occasions when he relaxed, he read the Chinese newspaper he subscribed to and enjoyed hunting and fishing.

Picnics and outings were a frequent family event. On July 4, 1920, everyone went to Nogales to spend the day, except Carmen, who was pregnant. What's now an hour's trip down the interstate was then a half-day endeavor. The cars' narrow tires had so much trouble negotiating the deep sandy wash at Canoa Ranch that a windlass was installed on each side and all the cars were winched across.

That afternoon, Carmen Lee Ban's first child, Edward, was born, with the help of a local midwife.

Soon afterward, those years of working in her mother's stores paid off, for she and her husband opened the first of what would be a series of four grocery stores. "They worked very long hours," Edward recalled. "My father would get up around four a.m. and go to the market to pick out the vegetables and meat. He was also the butcher, so he'd trim all the meat and all the produce and arrange the display. My mother was the mastermind, and she did all the accounting."

The last family grocery, like the others, was in midtown Tucson. Unlike the others, it was next door to a large and prosperous Safeway food store, but Edward said the two coexisted peacefully. They catered to different markets, and competition wasn't a problem.

Throughout the early 1920s, in addition to working in the grocery stores, Carmen kept her interest in photography and was employed as a retoucher at the Elite Studio. She also worked for Buehman & Co. Photographers.

There's certainly no doubt that Carmen and Ban Sing worked hard and long, but their photo albums document good times as well. The extended family remained close, and the photographs from the next ten years show gatherings of thirty or forty relatives at picnics, reunions, and get-togethers. Many weekends found the family loading baskets and boxes of food into the Packard to head to somewhere cooler and shadier than the city. Pets were an important part of the family, and Blackie, a black-and-white cocker spaniel, along with a series of cats, appears in many of the pictures. Rarely, it seems, was Carmen without her camera, a folding Kodak.

The reunion tradition continues today, and a 1990s photograph hangs on Edward Ban's wall, showing more than one hundred relatives all gathered at a Tucson park.

Tragically, Carmen died at her Tucson home November 14, 1940, at the young age of forty-nine, not from uterine cancer, but as a result of the radiation burns from its treatment.

All the Chinese exclusion laws were still in effect at the time of her death and weren't repealed until 1943. Officially, no more than 105 Chinese per year were allowed to immigrate to the country until that law was abolished by the 1965 Immigration Act.

POLINGAYSI QÖYAWAYMA

(1892–1990)
"BUTTERFLY SITTING AMONG THE FLOWERS IN THE BREEZE"

A bitter wind whipped through the brown, frost-burned Kansas cornstalks that morning in 1910. The air was brisk and cold enough that the two people entering the restaurant were glad of the establishment's warmth.

The woman, wrapped in a shawl and long cotton dress, was tiny, less than five feet tall and barely ninety pounds. Her dark eyes focused shyly on the floor, and her black hair was long, except for the bangs cut straight across her forehead. The man was tall, slender, dignified, and dressed in a dark suit. A Bible peeked out of his jacket pocket.

They stood near the doorway, an incongruous pair, before finding an empty table, and talked quietly about looking forward to something hot to drink.

The waitress, a surly, stout woman in a too-tight dress, walked past them, then paused to stare at the woman. She growled, "We don't serve colored."

The seated woman looked perplexed.

The man's mouth tightened, but his voice remained soft and polite. "My name is Reverend Jacob Frey. This is Elizabeth Ruth Qöyawayma, an American Indian visiting from Arizona. If you won't serve us, I'd like to speak to the manager."

The manager appeared, and the two men argued until the young woman suddenly rose from her seat, tears sliding down her face.

"Please, please, can we leave?" she begged the missionary. "I don't want to eat here. I couldn't swallow the food."

Polingaysi Qöyawayma Used by permission of Al Qöyawayma

❧

This incident was all too symbolic of Polingaysi Qöyawayma's life. No matter where she traveled, she seemed to fall between cultures. Many years later she would write: "What can one do about one's skin? We, who are clay blended by the Master Potter, come from the kiln of Creation in many hues. How can people say one skin is colored, when each has its own coloration? What should it matter that one bowl is dark and the other pale, if each is of good design and serves its purpose well?"

Eventually, she was able to accept and relish the traditions of her original culture and use them to help her people bridge the gap between their ways and those of the white man.

Polingaysi Qöyawayma was born in the Oraibi Pueblo on the Hopi Reservation in northeastern Arizona. Her name (pronounced Poe-LING-[slight pause]-nigh-she, Ko-YAH-[slight pause]-why-mah) translates to "Butterfly Sitting among the Flowers in the Breeze." The Hopis didn't keep track of dates, but she's said to have been born in the spring of 1892.

Spirituality is a vital part of Hopi life. As Polingaysi would later tell her biographer, their "religion was not a Sunday affair; it was a daily, hourly, constant communion with the Source, the Creator from whom came all things that were, large or small, animate or inanimate, the power behind Cloud People, Rain People, the Katsina, and all the other forces recognized and respected by the Hopi people."

Despite this deep faith, white missionaries considered all Native Americans to be sinful and in need of salvation. In the late 1880s, they began moving onto the reservations, determined to convert the "heathens."

Polingaysi's father, a member of the Badger Clan, worked for H. R. Voth, a Mennonite missionary who moved to Oraibi in 1893. "Qöyawayma" was too much of a tongue-tangler for English speakers, so the missionary simply called him Fred.

Reverend Voth was a kind man who recognized Fred's quick intelligence. He taught Fred carpentry and how to deliver babies and pull teeth. Fred also accompanied the minister on several trips to Kansas, an experience that would provide him with some perspective on why his daughter might someday want to follow the white man's way.

Polingaysi's mother, Sevenka, was a hard-working woman who had a beautiful singing voice. She was also deeply devout and, according to later accounts, lived by this philosophy: "We do not walk alone, Great Being walks beside us, Always know this, And be Grateful." She passed her musical ability on to her daughter, along with her connection to the Coyote Clan, descendants of the ancient Anasazi Pueblo of Sikyatki. Sevenka saw no reason to leave either the village or her adopted Hopi ways, and her conservative opinions would prove to be a source of friction between her and her daughter.

Records and artifacts show that the Hopi people and their predecessors have occupied the area since AD 500, longer than any other Native American tribe in the United States. Their homeland, or tutsqua, originally covered eighteen million acres, but now the Hopis have only 9 percent of their original holdings, and their land is surrounded by the Navajo reservation.

The Hopi leaders eventually established their villages on the mesas, which were named by early explorers—with a surprising lack of originality—First Mesa, Second Mesa, and Third Mesa. Oraibi was the first village on the Third Mesa, and because they were first to arrive, members of the Bear Clan were considered the leaders.

In the late 1890s government officials, along with the help of Navajo policemen, searched the houses of the Hopis, saying the children must go to school to learn the ways of the predominantly white culture—and unlearn their own. If the adults had enough warning, they hid the children. If not, the boys and girls were dragged off, screaming and crying, to the school building.

The Hopi families of Oraibi were intensely divided between the progressives, who believed the tribe should give in to the white man's way, and the conservatives, who said, "When a Hopi becomes a white man [takes on Caucasian ways], he no longer has a face. We want to be Hopis, not white men. We want our children to learn Hopi ways and live by them."

No matter which side the parents chose, soon most of the village children were in school—but not Polingaysi. Not only was she lonely, but she also noticed that her friends returned to the mesa at the end of each day apparently unharmed, and often they were even laughing.

If this development already interested her, the final enticement was when she learned the school day included lunch.

Even though Polingaysi knew her family would be angry and wounded, her curiosity drove her down off the mesa and into the school of her own free will. There she was given a bath, a new dress, and a meal consisting of a saucer of syrup and a piece of hardtack. The teacher handed her a pencil and she set to work, diligently reproducing the odd-looking marks she saw on the board.

That afternoon, when Sevenka realized that her daughter had willingly gone to school, she said, "You have taken a step in the wrong direction. A step away from your Hopi people. You have brought grief to us. To me, to your father, and to your grandparents. Now you must continue to go to school each day. You have brought this thing upon yourself, and there is no turning back."

Those words were prophetic of the intercultural war that Polingaysi would feel in her soul for many years to come. In fact, her biography, published six decades later, carried the title No Turning Back: A Hopi Indian Woman's Struggle to Live in Two Worlds.

It was a conflict that affected not just her, but all Hopis. The festering and simmering split between the progressives and the conservatives boiled over September 6, 1906, when the Bear Clan forced out those in the conservative Spider Clan, which marked the establishment of Hotevilla and Bakavi. The dispute had a bitter ending for all, with no clear winners. Oraibi lost its heart, and year by year, more families left. The Qöyawaymas moved to a house in New Oraibi, now called Kykotsmovi, at the bottom of the mesa near the government school.

Polingaysi continued to attend school and soon found that academic work was easy, and that she was hungry for more learning. Later that same year, her own life became as fractured as that of her people.

Many of her friends were attending the Sherman Institute in Riverside, California, an off-reservation boarding school for Indian children. After much begging on her part, her parents relented and let her go. Her years at Sherman were lonely ones, but she studied hard and continued the musical training she'd begun in the government school.

In 1910 Polingaysi returned to her village only to realize how far she'd drifted culturally. According to her biography: "Polingaysi looked at the little house and the windswept yard where chickens pecked at bits of grain. The poverty of the scene made her heartsick. This life was not for her. She would never again be happy in the old pattern. She had gone too far along the path of the white man."

After four years of schooling, she preferred eating from a table to sitting on the floor, and she wanted to sleep in a bed. She wanted to cook lavish pies and cakes instead of cornmeal, and, as one who'd recently adopted the Christian faith, she tried hard to persuade her family to abandon their native beliefs. No part of her attitude won her any fans in the community, and she became increasingly unhappy. But at the same time, she was still Hopi in her heart, and she loved her family and village and wanted some way to sink roots back into her community.

Fortunately, her father saw a potential solution and arranged for her to live with the new missionary, Reverend Jacob Frey, and his family in Moenkopi, about forty miles from New Oraibi.

Before taking her there, however, he led her to a plot of land about half a mile from the family's house, where he'd planted a thriving young cottonwood tree. Here, Fred Qöyawayma told Polingaysi, was a place that was hers to build on. Like the cottonwood, she too would have a place to sink her roots. From that moment on she resolved to work hard and save money to build a house on that very spot.

The Freys made Polingaysi, whom they called Elizabeth Ruth, a part of their Mennonite family and provided opportunities for work, travel, and exposure to new experiences. A trip to Newton, Kansas, was particularly significant. It was there that she learned about discrimination when refused service at a restaurant. But it was also where Bethel Academy (now Bethel College) inspired her to continue her education as a Mennonite missionary.

The following year, 1911, she started school at Bethel, financing her tuition, room, and board by working in the kitchen and dining room.

By 1918 Polingaysi had finished college and started missionary work, but she realized that in spite of her accomplishments, she was restless and dissatisfied. The Hopis were happy with their own spiritual lives, and despite her missionary training, part of her agreed with them and saw no reason to influence them to change their faith.

In September she was asked to take a position of teaching assistant in the Kayenta Indian boarding school, near the Utah state line and Monument Valley. Oddly enough, because she never even started the job, the opportunity would change the course of her life.

She traveled to Kayenta, but the day she was due to start her new position, the influenza epidemic sweeping the world hit the nearby town of Tuba City, and she was needed to help care for the sick. She too came down with the disease and was hospitalized. She survived, unlike six hundred thousand Americans, including hundreds of Hopis and Navajos.

After her recovery she was offered a position at the Tuba City boarding school and worked there as a substitute teacher for one term.

Still thinking that her doubts about being a missionary meant she needed more education, she moved to California to attend the Los Angeles Bible Institute. After two years she returned to the reservation to at last begin building the house of her dreams under the cottonwood tree.

In 1924 the government day school at Hotevilla offered her a position as housekeeper. She was torn: The job would bring a steady paycheck that would help pay for her house—and it was an alternative to mission work. Despite her concern that the Freys and her other Mennonite friends would be shocked and hurt, she nonetheless took the offer with relief. She also worried that the Hopis of Hotevilla would not accept her. She had, after all, urged them to give up their culture. Besides, they were descendants of those who had been ejected from the original village in 1906, and she feared they might resent her Oraibi origins.

Thanks to Polingaysi's solid work ethic and cheerful disposition, she was not only accepted by the other Hopis, but soon school officials asked her to teach the first-grade children. She'd never taken the government service examination, nor had she any formal teaching credentials, and school policy prohibited the use of the Hopi language. Yet, she found a way to connect with the children while teaching them English. Hopi stories and legends became the bridge between cultures and a basis for a vocabulary built of simple familiar things from home. Within a few months her students could spell simple words, count, and even speak whole sentences in English.

With that success Polingaysi began to feel as if she'd found her place between the two cultures she'd been straddling and to understand the vital role education played in the process.

I tell the young people this: "Your foundation is in your parents and your home, as well as in your Hopi culture pattern. Evaluate the best there is in your own culture and hang onto it, for it will always be foremost in your life; but do not fail to take also the best from the other cultures to blend with what you already have. We are not a boastful people, so do not allow your educational advantages to make you feel contempt for the older ones of no education who have made your progress possible. Give them credit for the good that is in them and for the love they have in their hearts for you. Don't boast, but on the other hand, don't set limitations on yourself. If you want more and still more education, reach out for it without fear. You have in you the qualities of persistence and endurance. Use them."

Within a year she passed the U.S. Indian Service test to become a full-time government employee. Still determined to further her undergraduate education, she spent the summer taking classes at the teaching college in Flagstaff, side by side with white schoolteachers.

After several years of teaching, she was transferred to Chinle, then Toadlena, New Mexico, to teach Navajo children.

By this time Polingaysi was approaching forty and longed for children of her own. She had become friends with a part-Cherokee man, and, in the spring of 1931, she and Lloyd White were married at the Bloomfield Trading Post in Toadlena. She also received the good news that she'd been transferred back to Hopiland and would be teaching in the Hopi village of Polacca in the fall.

The couple spent the summer in Oraibi, where they received a warm welcome from Polingaysi's parents, although many others in the community disapproved of her marrying outside the Hopi tribe. Soon, deep disagreements divided the newlyweds, and the marriage ended— without children—within a couple of years.

In the meantime Polingaysi had been adding rooms to her house. Music and singing had always provided a soul-satisfying emotional refuge for her, and at last she had a home for her piano. She also had sufficient room to take in paying guests during summer vacations. There was nowhere else to stay in Hopiland, and many politicians, anthropologists, and writers enjoyed her hospitality for the next three or four decades. Theodore Roosevelt and Ernest Hemingway were but two of her guests.

After two terms of teaching at Polacca, she was again transferred, at last to her home ground of Kykotsmovi, the former New Oraibi. It was a mixed blessing—she was home, close to her family and friends, but she still had to face resentment and rejection by some in her community.

She became silent, introspective, brooding. Once more she was trapped in a spiderweb structure of suspicion, based on her own fears. The more she tried to push it away, the more entangled she became. The sense of rejection that had haunted her all her life bowed her spirit down with grief. Because of her Hopi heritage, she told herself, she would never be fully accepted by the white world, and her own Hopi people resented her interest in the world and her ability to work in it. Which way could she turn?

Ironically, relying on that very combination of cultures—the Hopi tradition of nonresistance and the comfort of her Christian faith—helped ease her out of the depression. In addition, her teaching methods had gained national attention and honors. In 1941 she was chosen from all the U.S. Indian Service teachers to demonstrate to school officials from around the continent her way of teaching Indian children, using their own traditions.

She also wrote a children's book, The Sun Girl, about a young Hopi girl who has to make a difficult choice between her grandparents. The book earned her the Arizona Author Award from the Arizona State Library Association and the Libraries Limited Group.

In the late 1940s Fred Qöyawayma developed diabetes and moved into Polingaysi's home, where she could provide the nursing care he needed. He, of all people, understood her best, and she missed him terribly when he died. Soon, Sevenka's health failed as well, and she died in 1951.

By 1954 Polingaysi was more than sixty years old and ready to retire from teaching. To her surprise, her retirement celebration drew hundreds of friends and former students—as well as a bronze medal of commendation and the Distinguished Service Award from the U.S. Department of the Interior.

Never one to lapse into inactivity, Polingaysi launched herself into a new life of music, art, and writing, while continuing to help her Hopi people. She set up a scholarship fund for Hopi students that continues today at Northern Arizona University. She began working with clay and created beautiful pots in a style all her own, with raised symbols on a soft pink clay, reminiscent of her native mesas. Some of her pots are in a permanent collection at Phoenix's prestigious Heard Museum.

Her artistic and educational legacies live on through the work of the nephew she mentored, Al Qöyawayma. Like his aunt, he too is a bridge between worlds, although in his case he straddles art and science, as well as tribal traditions and contemporary high-tech environments. He is both a gifted ceramicist, whose work has been featured internationally, and an engineer with patents in high-tech guidance systems for commercial and military aircraft and airborne star trackers. But what might please Polingaysi the most is that her nephew cofounded the American Indian Science and Engineering Society, which funds scholarships for indigenous peoples. As of 2011, the society had more than twelve thousand alumni over three decades, as well as about three thousand current members.

The early 1970s were difficult for Polingaysi. Not only was she almost killed in 1972 when hit by a pickup truck, but the house that meant so much to her was destroyed by fire in 1974, along with everything in it, including her beloved piano. Two years later, thanks to family and friends, the house was rebuilt, and she was able to go back to pottery and her other activities.

Recognition for her accomplishments continued to flow in, and in 1976 the Museum of Northern Arizona asked the famed sculptor Una Hanbury to do a bronze sculpture of Polingaysi. Bethel College recognized her as 1979's Outstanding Alumna, and during the next few years, she also was awarded the Arizona Indian Living Treasure tribute, the Heard Museum's Gold Medal, and Bullock's national "Be Beautiful" Award.

Polingaysi was fortunate to remain healthy into her eighties, but in 1981 she suffered a stroke and soon needed home health care. In 1989 she grew so frail that she had to move from New Oraibi to a Phoenix nursing home. She died there on December 6, 1990.

In 1991 she was included in the Arizona Women's Hall of Fame. In a 2002 interview, Al Qöyawayma said of his aunt:

There are people who transcend their culture. It doesn't matter if she'd been born in Russia, in China, or here. She would have been something different, but she would have still been a force. There are two kinds of forces. One comes up against a mountain, yells, screams, and brings in the earth movers. The other comes up against a mountain, puts a hand on it—and the mountain begins to move. That was her.

LUISA RONSTADT ESPINEL

(1892–1963)

ARTISTIC INTERPRETER OF
SPANISH CULTURE

Lingering darkness wrapped the thick adobe walls of the Tucson house, but the smell of fresh tortillas, along with the clatter of kitchen noise and chatter of voices, awakened the sleeping child. She stirred, stretched, and was suddenly wide awake. This was no time to lie around—it was a picnic day!

She smiled with anticipation in the dark. The hot summer sun would still lie below the Rincon Mountains when all the aunts, uncles, cousins, more cousins, and friends from all over town would load baskets of food and piles of musical instruments into horse-drawn carriages and wagons. Two hours later, they'd all convene where the creek flowed out of Sabino Canyon, or maybe in the shade of the trees near San Xavier, or perhaps under the cottonwoods of Oracle.

Gunshots would rip the early morning air as the men hunted, while the women, with less than useful help from the children, unpacked the baskets. The men would return, guns over their shoulders, their furred and feathered prey dangling. The aroma of cooking meat would blend with those of coffee and wood smoke, and finally everyone would settle down to a picnic breakfast, with fresh rabbit or quail or dove, accompanied by a rich familial sauce of laughter, gossip, teasing, and talk.

Then would come the music, and she knew her father and all the parientes (relatives) would sing and play the guitar for hours. Eventually, the sun would sink behind the jagged Tucson Mountains, a signal for everyone to pack up the empty baskets and drift back to the town, some still singing quietly as the children slept.

Luisa Ronstadt Espinel Arizona Historical Society, Tucson, AHS # 69493

Luisa Ronstadt scrambled out of bed, shook her little sisters awake, and began hastily to dress.

⁊

Much of the early history of Arizona pioneers is really a family story. Towns were small, the same names appear again and again, and when reading old journals, it seems as if everyone was related to everyone else, either by blood or by marriage, and sometimes both. The border between Arizona and Mexico sometimes seems fuzzy—which indeed it was until it was marked and surveyed in 1855. Even afterward, the bonds between families were far stronger than the lines between nations. That was especially true of the old Mexican families, and the names of Redondo, Elias, Urrea, and Vasquez are still common on both sides of the border.

Probably no story illustrates this better than that of the family of Luisa Ronstadt.

Colonel Frederick Augustus Ronstadt, Luisa's grandfather, was born in Hanover, Germany, in 1819. A mining engineer, he worked and traveled through South America, eventually arriving in Mexico, where he became a naturalized citizen in 1843. He married during a twenty-three-year military career with the Sonora National Guard, but his wife died while their four children were still very young. In 1867 he married Margarita Redondo of Altar, whose family came from Spain to settle Sonora in 1790.

They had three children, and the first, Federico José María Ronstadt, later known to all his friends as "Fred," was born in Las Delicias, Sonora, Mexico, north of Hermosillo, in 1868. The colonel and his wife were parents who cared about education and culture. By the time young Fred was fourteen, he had read all the novels of Alexandre Dumas in Spanish and could read and write English as well. Even as a youngster, the boy had obvious and considerable musical ability, and his parents arranged for him to have flute lessons.

147

In a parallel story, Alexander Levin, born in Bahn, Prussia, was one of the early Jewish pioneers who arrived in southern Arizona soon after the Civil War. He married Zenona Molina, also from an old Sonora family. Alex was a brewer and a wise businessman who foresaw the demand for a cold beer in Tucson's hot climate. In 1869 he established Levin's Park, a three-acre precursor to the amusement park, featuring a restaurant, riding stable, theater, opera house, dance pavilion, and even an archery range.

He and Zenona also had a daughter, Sara, who would marry Federico Ronstadt. Luisa would be the Ronstadts' first child.

But a decade before that wedding, Colonel Ronstadt brought fourteen-year-old Fred to Tucson in April 1882. The Southern Pacific Railroad had arrived in 1880, an event that's been described as a "social and economic volcano," but many goods were still hauled by mule and wagon. Tucson had no less than four wagon makers, and Fred's parents resolved he would learn the business at the firm of Dalton and Vasquez. Mrs. Dalton was a cousin of Fred's mother, which gave him a family to live with during his apprenticeship.

(Interestingly, several months after Fred's arrival, he was sent at midnight for the midwife to deliver Mrs. Dalton's fourth baby. That child was Lupe Dalton—who twenty-two years later would become Fred's second wife and the mother of their four sons.)

Fred's days as an apprentice were long ones, but soon after his arrival, he found himself spending time with the Levin family. In his memoir, Borderman, he wrote about discovering his former music teacher at Levin's Park and playing with the orchestra until midnight. The next morning he was informed by the Daltons in no uncertain terms that hanging out with musicians at the beer park was not considered acceptable behavior.

Fred was a hard worker and a quick study, and at nineteen he bought the wagon shop where he'd apprenticed. He moved his father, mother, and three younger siblings from Mexico to Tucson, where Colonel Ronstadt died in 1889. Soon, Fred prospered to the point where Ronstadt wagons rolled down roads from northern Colorado to southern Sonora.

In 1890, Federico married Alexander Levin's daughter, Sara. Two years later Luisa was born, to be followed by Laura, Fred, and Alicia.

The family only spoke Spanish at home, and Luisa didn't learn English until she went to school. Music, on the other hand, was always a part of her life. Her mother played the piano, her sisters and brother sang, but it was her father who had the most influence over her musical life. Years later, she told the Arizona Daily Star:

> *There were other summer evenings I remember when the moon shadows of the grape leaves latticed the arbor, and my father sitting there, his face illumined, would accompany his songs on his guitar and later tell us stories of when he was a little boy. . . . The most vivid memories of my childhood are interwoven with music and mostly the music of my father, who loved it. It was his whole life in those days; his business was a secondary consideration.*

When she was about six, her father formed one of the town's first orchestras, Club Filarmónico Tucsonense. Years later, she recalled "being allowed to attend the long rehearsals with my mother, and when they were over, being too tired and sleepy to walk home, my father used to carry me on his shoulders and tuck me into bed." The orchestra, which lasted until 1905, was a highlight of Tucson social life, and even traveled to southern California on tour.

In 1902, when Luisa was ten, a scarlet fever epidemic struck Tucson, killing her mother, Sara, who was pregnant with a fifth child. A couple of years later, Lupe Dalton, then twenty-two, needed a job and came to the Ronstadt Company as a bookkeeper. She and Fred fell in love and were married on Valentine's Day, 1904.

Soon, Luisa had four half-brothers: William, Alfred, Gilbert, and Edward. They were all musically gifted as well, and they would produce yet another generation of singers, songwriters, and instrumentalists. Many of them are still frequent performers; the most well known is Gilbert Ronstadt's daughter, Linda.

Luisa's musical education continued at boarding school, and around 1911 she moved to San Francisco to study, take voice lessons, and work as an organist. She also began the research that would change the direction of her life. While browsing in the library of Juan Cebrian, a noted scholar of Hispanic history, she ran across a collection of songs and legends that she'd often heard as a child. According to a music critic for the Los Angeles Times: "The discovery of these familiar things in a new and glamorous setting was a definite experience to her. It gave them a sudden new life in her imagination and stimulated her desire to explore further into their background. Eventually it turned the course of her music career away from conventional channels."

She moved to Georgia and taught music at Lucy Cobb College in Athens. Later, she taught at Georgia Teachers College. It would be another decade before she realized the impact she had on the South.

In April 1917 she returned to Tucson and performed the role of Azucena in Verdi's Il Trovatore at the Saturday Morning Music Club to raise funds for the Temple of Music and Art. By now, she had taken the stage name "Luisa Espinel." Her voice was mature and was sometimes described as a mezzo soprano, sometimes as a contralto. One reviewer described it as "magnetic, husky, deep, resonant: and [sic] instrument with which she plays on her listeners' emotions. . . . Then there is the matter of her singing voice. In this, too, there is depth, richness, the same husky quality as in the spoken voice, but more." In 1924 she traveled to Europe in search of more folk songs and spent two years in Spain and one in France. She wrote long and affectionate letters to her parents, and one 1925 message from Toledo, Spain, shows she had a gift for language as well as for music:

Robert took us way upon the hill overlooking Toledo, so that we could get a view of the sunset. It was unforgettably lovely. Here I must say again that it reminded me of the Arizona sunsets, also its surroundings were like Arizona—arid and rocky. We could hear the noises of the city like a faint murmur, accompanied by the monotonous and regular splash of the water from the river on the rocks—the wind broke the occasional sound of a guitar, and at longer intervals the broken strains of a song. It was beautiful and wonderful to have the privilege of sitting on those rocks high above that ancient city and hear its old heart throb, and to hear the monotonous rythmatic [sic] music of the Tajos that has guarded it for so many centuries.

Again, she mentions her love of Arizona in another letter several days later:

The Castillian landscape has such character—it is severe, but it has such strength and virility that it makes up for its aridness— maybe it is because it all reminds me of Arizona—and after all one can't help but feel a great affection for the landscape around one's home town. Today the Manzanares looked just like the Santa Cruz looks around about Nogales. The populars [sic] here could be compared to the cottonwoods there.—Of course, there are more trees here, but it's ever so much alike.

During her time in Spain, she fine-tuned her act into a scholarly combination of music, acting, and dance. She researched the music she wanted to perform, spending weeks in museums, private libraries, the Spanish National Library in Madrid, and the Columbus Library in Seville. The songs and dances dated back to the late 1200s and featured music from Castile, Galicia, and Andalusia.

She also combed the countryside for instruments and costumes. According to the Tucson Citizen, the tambourine she eventually found "hung for one hundred years in an Asturian kitchen in northern Spain and was the property of a peasant girl, Gloria, with a reputation for magic." She also found a Valencian brocaded silk wedding dress that was more than a century old. The Citizen writer remarked, "The costumes and properties she uses would make in themselves a little museum."

The year 1927 brought her triumphant debut performance at the Edith Totten Theatre in New York City, along with four encores and a standing ovation. "Senorita Espinel can congratulate herself on a genuine success . . ." wrote a New York Times critic. "Her entertainment was interesting, unusual and artistic. She made a colorful figure in Spanish costumes and acted her songs naturally and wittily. . . . The Senorita . . . is a graceful dancer, as well as a talented singer."

But the compliment that pleased her the most came from the Los Angeles Times reviewer who noted, "Cognizant Spaniards declared it was the first time the folk music of Spain had been presented in its pure form, without the pernicious influence of Broadway or the boulevards of Paris."

The performance included an eight-page program with a preface that Luisa wrote herself. She described the wealth of Spanish folk music and the distinctiveness of the twelve regions, and then added:

> *To transplant folk-songs from their native background to a concert hall is like placing a bouquet of wild flowers in a drawing room—while still beautiful, they lose that essential grace which is let [sic] to them by open fields and hillsides. A song of Andalusia needs a patio, a garden, a guitar, and a brilliant sky. On the other hand, those from Galicia need the rugged mountains, the misty landscapes and the "gaita" and "tambor" to bring out the plaintive sweetness of their nostalgic melodies. I can only hope that in*

bringing this garland of wild flowers from Spain, I will be able to
suggest of the perfume that was theirs in the native land.

In November that same year, Luisa returned to Tucson to give a recital in her hometown and thrilled the already delighted audience by adding some Arizona and Mexican songs.

One writer began her review this way: "Sometimes you have a lovely dream from which you dislike to waken, but waking want to share it with those you meet. That is the way I felt about the program Luisa Espinel gave last night at the Temple of Music and Art." She went on: "You could not imagine just any singer singing these songs. . . . The costumes are delights, unusual, striking, so much a part of the program. The arrangement of the program itself is varied, always entertaining, but going beyond entertainment and appealing to every finer sense."

Luisa's career peaked in 1928. In April she returned to a warm welcome in Athens, Georgia, where she'd taught before going to Europe. She wrote to her father: "I never realized what a great number of loyal friends I had here in Athens. The town turned itself inside out to welcome me, and all my old pupils and friends have entertained as only southerners can. My concert here was a great success."

She was soon to receive a much greater honor. Mrs. Elizabeth Sprague Coolidge (no relation to Calvin) was a patron of classical twentieth-century music. Born in 1864, she was a talented pianist and wanted to perform, but that was too scandalous a career goal in her upper-class Victorian milieu. Instead, she married and founded a music school in her home in Pittsfield, Massachusetts. After the deaths of her husband and both parents, she faced the most tragic blow for a music lover, her own deafness. Yet, beginning in 1918, she established the Berkshire Festival of Chamber Music in Pittsfield (which continues to live on as South Mountain Concerts and is housed in the same 440-seat music hall). The festival was a highly prestigious three-day event, with morning and evening concerts featuring visiting musicians considered by Mrs. Coolidge to be worthy.

In 1928 Luisa was invited to join those musicians in Pittsfield, where she was the first singer of folk songs to appear at the event. She also performed at the Congressional Library in Washington, D.C.

She continued touring and spent 1932 doing a performance she called "Cuadro Castizos," or "little framed canvases of real life." One professor in Baylor University's Department of Spanish described her as "the only artist I know today who has lifted the classic folk ballads of Spain in all their literary and musical purity to the realm of the modern theatre and by her superb artistry makes of them fascinating entertainment."

She continued performing on the West Coast and once shared billing with piano virtuoso Vladimir Horowitz. She then settled in Los Angeles and moved into film, costarring several times with her friend Marlene Dietrich.

In 1934 she married Charles Kassler Jr., who was a painter, printmaker, and lithographer—in spite of having lost one hand in a high school chemistry experiment. Like many artists during the Great Depression, he was employed by the Works Progress Administration (WPA) and painted the two largest frescoes ever done under the WPA. One, Pastoral California, in Plummer Auditorium in Fullerton, California, is 1,200 square feet and features a banquet scene in which a popular singer of the time, Laura Moya, is entertaining. Appropriately enough, Luisa was the model for Laura Moya.

Four years later the fresco was whitewashed over, but in 1997 it was restored by high school students and community members.

The marriage ended after a short time, but Luisa remained in California, and she continued gathering her ancestors' songs that had never been written down before. Working with her father, she compiled them into a collection called "Canciones de Mi Padre" ("Songs of My Father"), which was published in 1946. Four decades later, her niece,

Linda Ronstadt, would release an album of the same name honoring her own father.

Luisa taught voice and gave private lessons to professional concert singers in the Los Angeles area until the early 1950s, when uncertain health forced her to retire. She continued teaching the public about Spanish traditions as the resident hostess at the historic Casa de Adobe historic mansion, part of the Southwest Museum.

On February 2, 1963, she died in Los Angeles.

But the musical tradition and the old songs of Spain and Mexico live on through the next generation. Many of her nieces and nephews continue performing.

How completely appropriate that in 1994 the City of Tucson awarded the Ronstadt family a Copper Letter award "for keeping the air of our town beautiful with song for well over a hundred years."

SARA PLUMMER LEMMON

(1836–1923)

BOTANIST AND ARTIST

A slight breeze lifted the brim of Sara's hat, carrying the creosote scent from the Sonoran Desert below. She paused to inhale deeply. Everything about southern Arizona was so different from what she knew in New England and coastal California: the light, the wildlife—and most certainly the plants.

Her shoulders ached from hefting the plant presses up the steep slope from the cave where she and JG were camped—and an unlady-like stream of sweat soaked her back as the fierce April sun beat down. She continued to stand gazing at the landscape spread out before her: the small settlement of Tucson below, the valley wrapped by the Rincon Mountains off to the east, the jagged Tucson Mountains to the west, and the Santa Rita Mountains to the south, still wreathed in light shreds of morning mist.

Above her, the mottled gray-brown cliffs of the Santa Catalina range stretched for the sky. Perhaps today she and JG would reach the peak? But even if they didn't, they'd find so many plants—most would be new to them, and indeed, new to the world of botany! She could hardly wait to capture them in watercolors.

Yes, she was hot. Yes, her muscles hurt. But the cough she'd been battling for months had abated, and finally feeling stronger was yet another reason to be grateful. As the descending notes of a canyon wren's song reverberated among the towering saguaros, she realized something.

She was deeply happy.

A rattle of loose rocks and an oath—quickly smothered—came from above her, and Sara didn't bother resisting a smile. Married just a few months earlier, they'd delayed their postnuptial trip until Arizona's growing season. Here, despite the hardships, her husband was as enthralled as she with discovering and preserving the plants they referred to as "new glories."

Yes, this honeymoon was indeed unusual!

Little did Sara know that some years later, in 1904, the 9,157-foot peak of this very mountain range would be named Mount Lemmon—in her honor.

⁓

Sara Allen Plummer was born on Saturday, September 3, 1836, in Gloucester, Maine. The family lived near Norman's Woe, the rock reef made famous in Henry Wadsworth Longfellow's poem "The Wreck of the Hesperus," written when Sara was four years old. Her father, Micajah Sawyer Plummer, started out in the grocery business but soon switched to full-time farming. Her mother, Betsey Haskell Plummer, tended to be sickly but still gave birth to Sara's two older brothers, her younger sister, and one younger brother, making Sara the middle child. Sara would remain close to her family, especially her sister Mattie, writing home nearly every single Sunday throughout her life.

Education mattered to Micajah and Betsey, who made sure the two girls went to a good private "female" college in Dover, Massachusetts. Sara became certified in teaching calisthenics, known to us today as gym class—even though as a child she'd always been prone to frequent colds and bronchitis.

In 1861, Sara moved to Brooklyn, New York, to attend the Greenleaf Female Institute, where she graduated with honors, doubly certified in chemistry and physics.

Then, in 1862, she was accepted to the Cooper Union for the Advancement of Science and Art. Established in 1859 by Peter Cooper, it was a remarkable educational institution that welcomed anyone who wanted to learn, regardless of their gender, race, or age. She studied chemistry and physics at night while teaching both calisthenics and private art lessons during the day.

Sara loved her life in New York City and spent every spare moment— what few she had—attending concerts, visiting art galleries, and socializing with poets, suffragettes, and other progressives. In addition, for three years she volunteered at New York's Bellevue Hospital as a nurse for wounded Civil War soldiers. Those skills would come in useful in the not-too-distant future.

Bellevue Hospital is also where she may have first crossed paths with Clara Barton, who would go on to establish the American Red Cross. As with teaching calisthenics, the choice of spending her spare time nursing is ironic, given her own terrible respiratory problems, particularly in wintertime. And then in 1863, she caught measles and nearly died. What was almost worse was having all her hair shaved to treat the pustules.

In 1870, pneumonia almost killed her, and she realized her life depended on escaping the bitter northeastern winters. She made the huge decision to move across the country, all by herself, to California— where she didn't know a single soul.

It was not an easy jaunt: the railroad wasn't reliable yet, so she went the long way around—from Manhattan south by steamship to Panama, by wagon over the isthmus, and then catching another steamship headed up the coast of Mexico and California. She finally disembarked in San Francisco where she stayed for a month before realizing her lungs weren't yet up to the Bay Area's cold and damp.

So she headed south to Santa Barbara, population 2,970. The climate was idyllic, especially compared to a New York winter, but she still wrestled with deciding if Santa Barbara was the place for her. She wrote the family, "Now I am at the jumping off place."

One problem with her new home was the lack of intellectual stimulation compared to New York City. And worse yet, there wasn't even a library!

"It's like death to me to be idle," she told Mattie as she rounded up donations from new California friends and old ones in New York. With the hundreds of books that arrived, she established Santa Barbara's first library, along with a small store that sold stationery and art supplies.

After a couple of years, the library lost its lease. Sara bought a small building where the library and store took up the front, and she moved into the back section.

Her health was still shaky, but she had built up her strength with long walks along the beach and in the hills above the town. She'd always been insatiably curious, and now she taught herself botany by making watercolor sketches of the local plants. She was also one of the founders of Santa Barbara's first natural history association. Since she still missed the stimulation of New York City, she initiated a lecture series in her library. That program might have been what attracted John Gill Lemmon to town in 1876—or perhaps it was the reputation of Santa Barbara's delicate, brown-eyed lady librarian.

John, who usually went by "JG," was born in Lima, Michigan, in 1832, four years before Sara. He became a teacher and then the county superintendent of schools. He'd been attending classes at the University of Michigan until hearing the call of war. He enlisted in the Union army in June 1862.

He participated in thirty-two battles in between stints of working as an army nurse or being hospitalized for injuries—until he was captured in August 1864. He was first held in Georgia's infamous Andersonville Prison and later the Florence Stockade in South Carolina, which if possible, was even worse. After two years of horrific POW treatment, JG was released in 1865. He wrote later that after a "year of liberal diet," his weight had increased to ninety pounds—this from a man who was six feet tall. Not surprisingly, these prison experiences left him permanently fragile with symptoms remarkably similar to those of posttraumatic stress disorder.

With his mother's help, he moved to Northern California to convalesce at his brother's home in Sierra Valley. JG had always been interested in botany, and during his recovery he started learning the western plants. The ones he didn't know he sent to Harvard University's Dr. Asa Gray, the preeminent American botanist.

The 1870s were a time of frenetic botanic activity. Many western plants still carry the names of the botanists of the time: Torrey pine, Engelmann spruce, Parry's agave, and more. All these men—John Torrey, Georg Engelmann, Charles Parry, and others—communicated frequently with one another and with Asa Gray. By this time Sara Plummer had educated herself to become a knowledgeable amateur botanist and illustrator, and both she and JG corresponded with them as well.

The two of them started botanizing together in the hills above Santa Barbara, always chaperoned by well-meaning friends, of course. One day Sara found a plant no one recognized, and JG sent it to Dr. Gray asking that it be named for her. To this day it's still known as Plummer's baccharis (*Baccharis plummerae*), in honor of her maiden name.

Already smitten, JG worked up the courage to propose to Sara. She agonized before refusing him, saying she loved him deeply but felt they were both too sick, too often, to marry. They remained affectionate pen pals for the next several years. Then, in 1880, Sara fell terribly ill with spinal meningitis and nearly died yet again. That brush with death apparently changed her mind.

Sara Allen Plummer and John Gill Lemmon were married on Thanksgiving Day, 1880, or as Sara described it to Mattie, they "plunged into the matrimonial vortex!" She was forty-four, he forty-eight. She relocated from Santa Barbara to Oakland and moved in with JG—and his mother. Fortunately, Sara was fond of "Dear Little Muzzer," and the trio formed a congenial, affectionate household. "Lemmonia" was Sara's pet name for JG, and he referred to her as "Amabilis," the species name of the pine tree that first enticed him into studying botany. The word also means "lovable" in Latin.

At Sara's suggestion, the couple resolved that, instead of "idling our time in useless saunterings, and listening to silly gossip," they would delay their honeymoon until the growing season when, as JG wrote, they would "make a grand botanical raid into Arizona, and try to touch the heart of Santa Catalina."

So in April 1881, Lemmonia and Amabilis arrived in Tucson by train and set up camp in the foothills north of the US Army's Fort Lowell. They spent two weeks struggling to get to the top of the range from the south side—and failed three times. They returned to town exhausted, but still determined.

Within a couple of weeks they communicated with Emerson Oliver Stratton who owned the Pandora Ranch, on the north side of the range. Stratton said he knew a route to the top and could even provide pack animals: "We went to the highest peak of the Santa Catalinas," he wrote later, "and christened it Mount Lemmon in honor of Mrs. Lemmon, who was the first white woman up there."

The Lemmons then traveled on to the Chiricahua Mountains in southeastern Arizona, but by then it was May and too hot for spring wildflowers. They returned to Oakland, renewed their railroad passes, and came back to the Arizona Territory that fall. Their Chiricahua expedition included three weeks in Rucker Canyon, eleven days of which they spent hiding from the Apaches in a tunnel with a crazed miner. He was most proud of setting up a line of dynamite with the intention, as he said, "to blow the Indians to smithereens."

During this trip, near what is now Fort Bowie National Monument, Sara discovered a yellow daisylike flower that turned out to be a new genus. Asa Gray named it *Plummera floribunda* in her honor; its common name is Apache Pass rubberweed, or less elegantly, sneezeweed.

Having not just a species but an entire genus named for her was a momentous taxonomic accomplishment, and Sara was overjoyed. She described her reaction in a letter to her father:

"I was so delighted with the honor—and such a fine plant—2 feet+ high, that I danced around our big herbarium, overturned the chairs, embraced L & Mother in the most enthusiastic way, and they joined me in the celebration."

Sadly, recent genetic examination shows the plant was not a new genus after all; it's now classified as *Hymenoxys ambigens*.

The following year they returned to Arizona, this time at the army fort in the Huachuca Mountains. Here they spent several months, calling it a "botanical paradise." Most of Sara's surviving artwork came from this time and place. She described their life to her family:

"I wish you could see our rough outfit of two gray/rubber blankets, old flannel vests & drawers, old boots & hats, a big lunch basket—filled with corned beef, crackers, cheese & three or four jars of nice currant jelly, brought in by good, thoughtful friends."

Three percent of Arizona's plants were discovered by this adventurous couple, many of which still carry the species name of "lemmonii." In 1884, Asa Gray made it clear that "whenever the name of Lemmon is cited for Arizonian plants, it, in fact, refers to the pair of most enthusiastic botanists." Plant species that still include Sara's maiden name are Plummer's onion (*Allium plummerae*), Plummer's candyleaf (*Stevia plummerae*), and Plummer's morning glory (*Ipomoea plummerae*).

In 1884, Sara was appointed as head of organizing the Pacific Slope section of what was known as the World's Industrial & Cotton Centennial Exposition—or the World's Fair. Again the couple boarded the train, this time bound for New Orleans and with hundreds of plant specimens and exhibits.

Sara Lemmon, in 1889 Photo by Wynne Brown. Original at University of
California & Jepson Herbaria Archives, University of California, Berkeley.

They stayed seven months there, enjoying their spare time by visiting with Clara Barton and her field agent Dr. Julian Hubbell.

Over the years they'd been frequent visitors to the San Luis Obispo area, and in 1886, they decided to homestead 160 acres near Cholame, California, (in sight of the intersection where James Dean would die in a car crash in 1955).

They first set up camp in a canvas tent—but the second day while they were out getting firewood, someone set fire to the tent, burning everything they had. Undaunted, they ordered wood from San Luis

Obispo and built a ten-foot-by-twelve-foot cabin by hand. Eventually, years later, they sold the land.

From then on, their lives were based in their Oakland herbarium, generally out in the field collecting plants during the growing season and eking out a living by selling specimens and seeds to collectors in the winters. They produced several botany books, illustrated by Sara, and did frequent botany lectures. How much of their work was done by JG and how much by Sara? No one will ever know, but several authorities believe that it was actually Sara who did much of the botanical work credited to JG because he remained so damaged by his war experience. Some, in fact, would include her among the world's early women pro-toecologists. Yet, as was typical of the times, the plant labels credit her work only as "JG Lemmon & Wife."

In 1895, they packed up their home and herbarium for the last time and moved to a tall house on Telegraph Avenue, not far from what is now the University of California's Berkeley campus. Sara loved the house with its sunlit rooms and ample space for her to paint, and to store so many of their books and specimens, and for them to host botanical and cultural events.

Women's clubs were a vital part of the social fabric, particularly in the realm of reform. Sara spoke often about the importance of forest conservation and also was frequently featured at women's suffrage events.

She was still active in the Red Cross and wrote the history of the Pacific Slope Red Cross. At 486 pages with dozens of photos, it was no small accomplishment. During this time she also quietly established the first training school for nurses on the West Coast—yet never mentioned it in any of her letters.

Some might say Sara Lemmon's most significant accomplishment was in 1903 when her ten-year battle culminated in the golden poppy being named California's state flower.

In June 1905, the Lemmons returned to Tucson, "hunted up" Emerson Stratton, and the following month the three of them retraced their steps on five burros in honor of JG and Sara's twenty-fifth anniversary.

She sent a postcard to Mattie, writing: "Both well & happy on this our Silver Wedding journey . . . We sleep in the open air beside a delicious mountain stream that sings our nightly lullaby."

She was sixty-eight, and he was seventy-three.

During their years together Sara had made hundreds of paintings, yet only a few remain. She was the second female member of the until-then all-male California Academy of Sciences—and the first woman allowed to speak to the group. After breaking through that barrier, she worked at the academy herbarium frequently, and she and JG often mentioned sending specimens and illustrations there.

At 5:12 a.m., April 18, 1906, the San Francisco earthquake convulsed the Bay Area and more. As if the earthquake wasn't bad enough, the fires that followed the quake gutted the California Academy of Sciences, destroying one hundred thousand specimens.

It's all too likely that Sara's paintings went up in flames as well.

Although she wrote a postcard to her family saying, "We are safe, tho' tremendously shaken," both Sara and John were shattered by the loss of so much of their work. JG's health, fragile at the best of times, continued to decline over the next year, and he lost much of his vision.

John Gill Lemmon died of pneumonia in November 1908, at the age of seventy-six, with his loving wife by his side. It was two days before their twenty-eighth wedding anniversary.

After JG was gone, Sara never really recovered—in fact, her sister Mattie believed that the trauma of the earthquake initiated her sister's mental decline. Gradually this distinguished, elegant, brilliant woman became "profane" and had to be physically prevented from leaving the house "unclad."

The family committed her to the Stockton State Hospital April 22, 1916, ironically on what years later would become Earth Day. The diagnosis was dementia.

Sara Allen Plummer Lemmon died January 15, 1923. She is buried with her Lemmonia in Mountain View Cemetery in Oakland, California, under a gravestone that reads, "Partners in Botany."

LAURA KERMAN

(1894–1999)

KEEPER OF HER PEOPLE'S CULTURE

For Tucsonans, El Día de San Juan is more than the Catholic tradition marking the feast day of St. John the Baptist.

In this town, nestled in the lap of the Sonoran Desert, June 24 celebrates the beginning of the monsoon season and its much-anticipated rain. Early in the month, billowing clouds begin to hover tantalizingly over the mountains. Sometimes they don't deliver. When rain doesn't fall, the desert doesn't turn green, few plants bear fruit, and residents groan about the "non-soon."

On June 24, 1983, Laura Kerman, a Tohono O'odham folk artist and storyteller, left her village of Topawa to visit the Tucson Botanical Gardens. She would be joining her friends, the staff of Native Seeds/SEARCH, as they celebrated ten years of preserving traditional seeds and farming techniques. Laura was in her eighties, still inquisitive about everything and enthusiastically active with a wide welcoming smile for all and a self-deprecating, merry sense of humor.

Being June in Tucson, it was a hot evening, still over one hundred degrees, and attendees fanned themselves and eyed the skies, hoping for rain that would break the heat. Laura explained the Tohono O'odham belief that June is when "the rain is getting ready way over the ocean. When it gets closer, it thunders and the ground shakes. After a while it rains here. It will moisten the whole ground, the whole world. Good for everything."

Laura then reached for her dried-gourd rattle, shook it a few times, and began to sing a rain song.

Within a few minutes, a breeze rustled the tops of the trees, the temperature dropped—and fat raindrops splattered on the flagstones.

∞

It could well have also rained Thursday, July 19, 1894, the day Laura Kerman was born, a day, as she described it years later, "before we knew the years had numbers."

In 1894, the tribe, known then as the Papago Indians, was seminomadic. In winter, the dry time, Laura's group of Papagos lived in sturdy cactus-rib-and-brush houses along streams in southern Arizona's Baboquivari Mountains, a "sky island" that juts up from the desert floor. In summer they moved down to the valley plains to grow the crops that would help sustain them for the next year.

The tribe's ancestral lands, *Papagueria*, stretched from the Gulf of California in northern Mexico, to the Gila River, a tributary of the Colorado River, in central Arizona. Their predecessors were the Hohokam (literally translated as "those who have gone before") who settled near the river pathways that wound their way through the Sonoran Desert: archeological evidence shows they were in the area for at least ten thousand years.

The Hohokam were early engineers, developing a canal system that snaked across the landscape for miles to irrigate the crops with rainwater despite the desert harshness. In 1878, by keeping those skills alive, the Papago Indians cultivated about twenty-five hundred acres of corn, tepary beans, sugarcane, and several kinds of squash.

Arizona has twenty-two Native American tribes, each recognized as its own sovereign nation by the American government. The 1854 Gadsden Purchase had separated southern Arizona from Mexico more than twenty years earlier—but no one informed the twenty-eight thousand actual residents that the land they'd been living on for centuries had been sold. As a result of the agreement, Laura's tribe still straddles the

US-Mexico border with enrolled members on both sides.

In January 1986 the Papagos changed their name from the Papago Tribe to the Tohono O'odham Nation, meaning "Desert People." They are closely related to the tribe living north of the Gila River, formerly known as the Pima Indians, now the Akimel O'odham, or "River People." To the west, near Ajo and Yuma, are the "Sand Dune People," or Hia C-eḍ O'odham.

All the O'odham have always been compatible, trading with another and visiting frequently—often on foot. Running was an important part of traditional tribal life as a way of delivering news, carrying prayers, competing in footraces, and as a ceremony. Sometimes the distance was short, but other times it wasn't, as the Salt Run rite of passage demonstrates: young men run from their home village to the Sea of Cortez (also called the Gulf of California)—a round trip of three hundred miles. Women of all ages had their own running game, as Laura remembered, competing in *tóka*, a game that resembles field hockey. It's still played with curved mesquite sticks and an *ola*, similar to a puck, fashioned out of two pieces of mesquite attached with deer gut.

Even today, the tribal newspaper is called the *Runner*.

The Tohono O'odham Nation is now primarily located on a 4,460-square-mile reservation in southern Arizona, the third largest in the United States, divided into four separate segments. This stretch of desert near Topawa is one of the hottest in the Southwest, with summer temperatures reaching well over one hundred degrees Fahrenheit. Rain, if it comes at all, arrives right around Laura's birthday, with violent thunderstorms that flush the arroyos, bringing water roaring down the sacred mountain, Baboquivari Peak, *Waw Giwulk*, before that welcome moisture fans out to flood the valleys.

Laura's earliest memories were of living with her family at *Keji:n e I wek*, or "Trees Grew Up," on the slopes of that mountain. Her parents were Juan and Guadalupe Laura Kerman, and she had three brothers—Andrew, Angelo, and Jose (pronounced "HO-see")— and one sister, Helen.

In the early 1900s, the US government decided the reservation needed more water, and it dug wells and installed pumps powered by windmills. That decision altered the flow of the tribal lives forever: no longer did they need to migrate to the mountains in winter to follow the water. Laura described the change: "Before the government put in the wells, there was nothing in the desert where Topawa is located. Nothing. Just all desert. Dry desert. Nothing. No. Before they had windmills where Topawa is, the people would come down after big rains and put little seeds in the ground and then go back to the mountains. There were no villages down here anywhere."

Her family then settled on land north of Topawa in the southeastern corner of the reservation and about seventy-five miles southwest of Tucson.

Her father still farmed using the floodwater technique, based on centuries of tradition and his own knowledge of soils and plants. "He would look at the big trees and he would look at little plants on the ground, and he found a little plant. In the hot weather time, everything was all dried up except that one little plant that was growing over there. There was still a little bit of green branches and leaves on that, and so he knew right there . . . if he softens it up, he'll reach a little moist ground."

Next, he planned the field carefully according to how much storm-water would flow down the wash and how it would spread out. Ecologists now know what the Hohokam knew generations ago: that floodwater is loaded with nitrogen, the most limited and most needed nutrient in arid-land farming. Juan built ditches and barricades to funnel the water to where he wanted it. "There are crops in different patches, that he knows where it's good soil for the corn and then he knows where there is good soil for the beans or the squashes. Yes, he knows all of that," said Laura in an oral biography.

As soon as the first rain softened the ground, it was all hands on deck for the whole family: "But what a job! We work in that all day long. Nobody can get away when the garden is to be worked. Oh no. Everybody works, girls and boys." In a good year, the growing season was about one hundred days, and families worked hard to dry the vegetables and store them in pottery jars and baskets.

No rain? No garden. May was the month when the stored food ran out—no wonder it was named *ko'ohk macat*, "the painful moon." So Laura's people still relied on wild foods provided by the desert, like the fruits of the saguaro, prickly pear, *pitahaya* (organ pipe) and barrel cactuses. Everyone welcomed June when the stately saguaro cactus bore its fruit, the first fresh produce of the year. The fruit was sweet, good for syrup and wine, and the seeds are full of oil: "Tiny little seeds," Laura explained. "They grind it, and then they put it in whatever they are cooking for themselves to eat. That was their lard."

In 1908, the Franciscan friars (OFM) began construction on the San Solano Mission, the parish headquarters. When not laboring in the garden with Juan, Guadalupe and Laura's younger brothers helped.

Most likely Laura wasn't part of that project because at the time she was living—with her parents' permission—at the US Industrial Indian School in Phoenix. It had been opened in 1891 for Pima and Maricopa boys because, as Indian commissioner Thomas Morgan announced at the opening, "It's cheaper to educate Indians than to kill them." In 1898 the school opened to other tribes, and in 1900 it housed 698 Indian students, the second-largest school in the nation.

Seventy years later, Laura still recalled a Papago policeman herding her and several other children onto a wagon and escorting them to Tucson. They traveled throughout the night since there was nowhere Indians were allowed to stop. The policeman then directed them onto a train where the children climbed onto the roof and held on for the 110-mile trip to Phoenix. There another wagon transported them to

Laura Kerman with one of her dogs at her home in view of Baboquivari Peak. Arizona State Museum, University of Arizona, Helga Teiwes, Photographer

the school. The staff separated girls from boys and then, one by one, as Laura recalled, took each girl "into the room with a little curtain over it. They stripped our clothes. We didn't have much clothes on anyway. They took our clothes off and turned on the . . . Oh I was afraid! They turned on the water!"

She found the clothes itchy and confining, and she especially detested the shoes, which, to a child whose feet had never worn more than the occasional deerhide sandals, were so tight they were torture.

No longer was time measured by the sun's passage through the sky. Blasts from a steam whistle announced the divisions of day and night and where and when she was expected to be. Mornings were for schoolwork, another challenge for a young girl who spoke not one word of English. In the afternoons she first learned to darn socks, then to sew button-holes, and eventually to make clothes. Other times she was assigned to the group of girls who were taught more of women's trades: how to set tables and polish silverware. Later she was moved to the laundry room to learn to wash and iron clothes.

In general, the Indian boarding schools were all about Anglo-conformity, and the students were taught the skills of laborers rather than leaders. All too frequently, when they went back to their reservation, they returned to a place that was no longer home, to a cultural no-man's-land of being neither white nor Indian. Some were even shunned by their own family, while at the same time lacking the tools to advance within a world run by white men.

Laura was miserably homesick at the school, so much so that at night it felt as if a hard rock had taken up residence in her chest. She missed her family, and as the sole Papago among Navajos and Apaches, she felt terribly alone. Eventually she met a Pima girl, whose language was at least similar to her own.

Her brother Andrew was also at the school for about a year until he ran away. After two years, Laura became so sick she was hospital-ized, and her father made the trip to bring her home. He borrowed a buggy and two horses, and after he gathered her and another girl who was returning to the reservation, they all traveled for hours each day. They paused only in places with enough grass and water for the horses and would sleep a few hours before continuing on. After several days, they reached Tucson, where Laura could see "the lights fly up into the sky"—and years later realized it must have been the Fourth of July.

To her great joy, her mother met them in Tucson. Juan returned the buggy to its owner, and for the last two days the family rode to Topawa without stopping. Her father used a thick, soft rope to secure the sleeping children so that they wouldn't slip off the horses.

Home. At last.

Laura remained in Topawa for the next couple of years, helping on the farm and housework. By now the community lived in adobe houses like their Mexican neighbors to the south; the circular brush houses of their ancestors, with mesquite or ironwood posts and saguaro ribs to support the roof, were a thing of the past.

She was a devout Catholic, and in 1911, a newcomer moved into the community who would have an enormous effect on her life. Father Bonaventure (Emil) Oblasser, OFM, a Franciscan friar and historian, arrived on foot to begin missionary work. He was known as "Desert Priest" or sometimes "Apostle of the Papagos." Soon he met Robert Humphrey Forbes, one of the early professors at the University of Arizona, in a history group. Dr. Forbes mentioned needing a young woman help his ailing wife, and Father Bonaventure recommended Laura. Her parents gave their permission, and thus began a fifty-year friendship among them all.

Laura's primary responsibility was caring for "Georgie" Forbes, and she soon referred to their house near campus as her second home. She credited them for teaching her English as well as how to buy vegetables from the Japanese vegetable merchants, cook the meals they liked—especially pies!—and keep house. She and the Forbeses became close, and the couple often invited her along when they traveled. In 1918, they moved temporarily to Egypt because Dr. Forbes was an agricultural consultant for the British government. They wanted Laura to accompany them, but her parents said no, that was TOO far from home!

The couple returned to Tucson in 1931, and Laura went back to work for them. Georgie died in 1946, and for the next twenty years

Laura divided her time between working for Dr. Forbes and, with guidance from Father Bonaventure and the local nuns, providing religious instruction to several different schools all over the reservation on both sides of the US-Mexico border. She never encountered anyone she liked enough to marry, but she adored working with children and thoroughly enjoyed teaching the rosary, prayers, and hymns in English, Papago, and Spanish.

In 1967, Father Bonaventure died and was buried in the Topawa cemetery.

The following year, Dr. Forbes died a few weeks shy of his one hundredth birthday—with Laura at his side. Later she said, "he fell and broke part of his body, and so he had to be sent to the hospital and to the home after."

Eventually the government took over public education on the reservation, and the mission schools closed, leaving Laura searching for something else to do. "I didn't know what to do with myself. I sit here. I lay there. I was lonesome. I first started basket making. Well, that went all right, but it was too hard to find straw way, way out."

So Laura Kerman reinvented herself as a potter and a storyteller.

She began with traditional pottery. Her grandmother had made pots for cooking and dishes and had shown her the nearby locations with the right kind of clay for different uses—and how to prepare it: "When you go to get the clay, you talk to the clay. Now people don't though, but I do. My grandmother taught me a song while she digs it. I would sit there and I sing for her until she gets it all."

Later she figured out how to combine the traditional techniques of pottery making with elements of contemporary ceramics, learning about clay slips and firing. She started making small figurines of the local desert animals and moved on to creating painted clay scenes of her people's traditional ways. Thus, for Laura, pottery became another tool for teaching and telling her people's stories.

Throughout the 1970s and 1980s, she continued teaching pottery and the ways of the Tohono O'odham culture, both to the reservation children and in Tucson schools. She welcomed visitors—and even whole classes—to her front yard, and she told stories, sang songs, and gave presentations throughout the state and beyond. She traveled to Salt Lake City, to a powwow in Montana, and went to other countries, including a visit to Guaymas, Mexico, with an opportunity to go fishing; to Montreal; and even journeying to Europe.

During this time she was also instrumental in seed keeping, the practice of banking traditional seeds. In 1983, the year Laura sang the rain song at the Tucson Botanical Gardens, the organization Native Seeds/SEARCH branched off from Meals for Millions. Its mission was—and still is—to collect and preserve traditional seeds from communities in the Southwest. Laura and her family were instrumental in donating some of the first preserved plant material in the organization's seed bank.

By 1989, Laura was in her nineties. She had returned from a prolonged stay in a Sells managed-care home and was gratefully back in her house, cooking and caring for her brother Jose. She then agreed to provide an oral history with her longtime friend Karen Reichhardt, a botanist turned library science graduate student. Laura was still working with clay, still teaching about her people's ways, and still the beneficiary of the desert. One friend, Robin Coon, who taught with Laura for years, recalls a "precious memory of sitting at her table under the soft glow of the night light, polishing our pots."

When Karen asked about using the creosote bush as herbal medicine, Laura told her about boiling the creosote leaves for sore feet and keeping the tea in the icebox. Anytime her feet ached, she'd heat the water, step into a bucket, and add the hot water. "I keep it as hot as I can. Then when it cools off, I warm it up again and put my feet in again, and then my blanket's ready, my bed's ready, and the second or the third time, I dry my feet and then I put on heavy socks, then I stick [them] under the blanket on my bed.

"By the morning, you can run a race to the mission—and back. Yes."

In 1999, Laura's race was over.

She died at age 105, out of sight of her beloved Baboquivari Peak, in a Tucson nursing home.

Ayra Hammonds Hackett

(1896–1932)
AFRICAN AMERICAN NEWSPAPER
FOUNDER AND EDITOR

Spring comes early in the low desert, and the morning of Wednesday, April 2, 1930, was warm—it was Phoenix, after all. And, like all weekdays, it had already been a busy one for Ayra Hackett. Getting her physician husband, Dr. Winston Hackett, out the door to the hospital he had founded and still managed, urging her thirteen-year-old daughter to be ready for school on time, reviewing all the plans for Sunday's young people's church tea.

No time to dally—time to get to work! she chided herself.

As she did several times a day, every day, Ayra paused before the framed picture of young John Prentice. He'd died five years earlier, at only six years old—and the pain of losing their only son still ripped her apart.

Briskly, she shook her head and sat down at her desk. The weekly deadline for the *Arizona Gleam*, the weekly community newspaper she established in their living room last year, was tomorrow. The three reporters—all women, she noted with a bit of unseemly pride—would be arriving any moment, and she still hadn't written her editorial column.

Again, she paused—and then began to type:

LIMITLESS
That's big talk—limitless. It covers a lot of territory. But so does life—and the opportunities that life gives us. So there is really no other word to describe the chances we have from the time we toddle to the time we totter. . . .

The Black population of Arizona was all too familiar with limits. In 1868, Mary Green arrived as the first recorded "Colored" resident in Phoenix. She came from Arkansas with her two children as a domestic servant of the former Confederate officer Columbus Gray.

At first Arizona lacked the Jim Crow policies that were so prevalent in the American South. But then in 1901, the Arizona Territory passed a law prohibiting "marriage of a person of Caucasian blood with a Negro or Mongolian," following the influx of Chinese American and African American men.

In March 1909, the territorial legislature passed a bill allowing segregation in school districts. The following year, Phoenix's population of 11,312 included 328 African Americans. Separation of races didn't just apply to schools: Blacks were forbidden to associate with whites in hospitals, restaurants, hotels, theaters, or buses.

By 1910, segregation had become a vivid daily reality: all sixteen Black students had to walk two miles to the one available high school, crossing carefully over the Southern Pacific and Santa Fe railroad tracks, every morning and afternoon.

The Phoenix residents of color didn't respond to the discrimination passively; instead they formed their own businesses, intellectual clubs, churches, political organizations, and media to keep their people informed. They also took care of their own, forming fraternal organizations to provide for the indigent, support education expenses, pay burial costs, and more. Associations including the Colored Masons, the Colored Odd Fellows, and the Colored Knights of the Pythias offered fellowship as well as a safe place for discussing and planning social reform and activism. Often the core of Black social life resided in secret societies including the United Brothers of Friendship and its women's auxiliary, Sisters of the Mysterious Ten. Hierarchies and rituals within the organizations, including coded door knocks and secret handshakes, were loosely based on the lodges and ceremonies of the Freemasons.

This was the social and cultural environment Ayra and Winston Hackett would be joining.

Named for her mother, Ayra was born in Winona, Texas, on March 29, 1896, to Elsie and Ayra Hammonds. Very little has survived about her childhood, but one newspaper account indicates she attended college and worked on the campus newspaper.

Winona is part of the Tyler metropolitan district, which is where Winston Clifton Hackett was also born and raised. He graduated from Tuskegee University in Tuskegee, Alabama, founded by Booker T. Washington, who was a prominent author, orator, and advisor to several American presidents. Winston Hackett then studied medicine at Meharry Medical College in Nashville, Tennessee, specializing in obstetrics.

Ayra and Winston married and moved to Phoenix, most likely because of its dry climate they hoped would improve Winston's respiratory issues.

They arrived in 1916 and set up home and office at 1334 E. Jefferson Street. The neighborhood, in what is now central Phoenix, was comfortable, mostly made up of professionals, including the principal of the Booker T. Washington School, who was married to the school librarian. Another neighbor was William Crump: he'd arrived in Phoenix in 1897 and worked as a waiter at the Ford Hotel before opening the Crump Hay and Grain Company. Now he sold citrus, barley, hay, and more to customers as far away as New York and San Francisco.

On the same street lived teacher Arthur Randolph Smith, who later founded the *Phoenix Tribune*, Arizona's first Black newspaper. In 1919, he wrote:

Phoenix is the best city in the U.S.A. . . . The most friendly relations exist between the Caucasians and the Colored people. Now

and then an antagonistic individual bobs up, but the good over-
whelms the bad until you scarcely realize any evil has been done.
. . . If you know all the real joy of living in a land that abounds
with figs, olives, peaches, apples, grapes, honey and all the good
things that were promised to the children of Israel if they obeyed
God, you must come to Arizona.

(Ironically, that same year the Phoenix Advancement League [PAL] was founded to fight discrimination, bigotry, and segregation. Two decades later it would become the first local branch of the NAACP.)

As Phoenix's first Black doctor and obstetrician, Dr. Winston Hackett was welcomed warmly. In Arizona, like most places at that time, all women relied on midwives to deliver their babies, and until World War II, most medical facilities in Phoenix were segregated. One exception was the Dana Maternity Home in Mesa, just outside Phoenix, which had been established by Helen Millett Grey Dana in her home in 1924. She ended up assisting or officiating at the delivery of more than 1,250 babies—babies of all ethnicities.

The Hacketts leapt into work, welcoming expectant mothers into their home, and Ayra quickly learned the skills she needed to help her husband deliver babies.

On June 15, 1917, she did more than help: one of the babies born in that house that day was their own as Ayra gave birth to their daughter, Winstona. A year later, on November 1, their son, John Prentice, was born.

By 1920, with two small children underfoot, Ayra must have been somewhat relieved that Winston had moved his office nearby to 32 N. First Street. Local advertisements read "Dr. W.C. Hackett, Physician and Surgeon: Special Attention Given To All Diseases Common to Men, Women, And Children. Confinements With Twilight If Desired." This description would have caught the attention of the town's pregnant ladies: "Twilight sleep" referred to the use of "scopolamin and morphin" to ease the pain of childbirth. One 1905 article described the mothers telling "of a sense of drowsiness stealing over them, a pleasant feeling of don't-care-ness, which finally merges into an overpowering sleepiness."

Despite energetic lobbying, Winston was unable to get funding for an African American community hospital. Instead he bought the house next door, which happened to be the residence of the former territorial governor, Joseph Kibbey. Perhaps Kibbey had an interest in a local hospital since ill health had driven him to Arizona in the 1800s. He was also a sympathetic neighbor. As governor, he had vetoed the 1909 territorial school segregation law because he believed it was unfair to give African American students an education that was "less effective, less complete, less convenient or less pleasant . . . than those accorded to pupils of the white race in the same district."

Several days later, the territorial legislature overrode his veto.

The summer of 1921 was an exciting time for both the neighborhood and the Hacketts. In June, Phoenix hosted its first Juneteenth Festival, commemorating the day in 1865 when federal troops arrived in Galveston, Texas, to ensure that all enslaved people be freed—even though the Emancipation Proclamation had been signed two years earlier. The festival took place in Eastlake Park and featured a hotly contested baseball game between Fort Huachuca's Tenth Cavalry and the local semipro team, the Western Giants.

Possibly, even more exciting was the July day that Dr. Hackett opened the private Booker T. Washington Memorial Hospital near the park and conveniently next door to his house. At first the hospital only had a few beds out on the screened-in porch. But Winston soon bought three adjoining lots, built six cottages for tuberculosis patients—and added "And Sanitarium Annex" to the title. The cost for a hospital stay ranged from $12.50 to $35 per week, and appointments were open to all, including indigents and those of all races diagnosed with "tawdry" disorders that required tactful and discreet treatment.

Winston also established a pharmacy and recruited Black nurses with college nursing degrees from southern schools.

By now the family was active among the social elite: Ayra belonged to the prestigious Black Women's Republican Club (BWRC) and was president of the Phoenix Federation of Colored Women's Club, in addition to being an active member of the Second Baptist Church where she hosted many teas for the congregation's young people. The same month the hospital opened, the *Phoenix Tribune* announced that she had been elected as "Worthy Princess" (president) of the Sisters of the Mysterious Ten.

Social reform and discrimination were frequent topics at dinner tables and association meetings. So everyone had to be worried when the *Phoenix Tribune* ran a front-page story with the headline, "Open Meeting of the Ku Klux Klan Realm of Arizona Held at Odd Fellows Hall in City of Phoenix." McCord Harrison, grand Kleagle of the Arizona Realm of the Knights of the Ku Klux Klan, read a short talk reminding attendees that all members must "be a believer of the tenets of the Christian religion, a believer in white supremacy, protection of American womanhood, prevention of the causes which lead to mob violence, that he must be a native born American who pledges allegiance to this government and its institutions."

In that same issue, the *Phoenix Tribune* published J. Ernestine Wyatt's poem "The Awakening." It opens with two verses that read:

There has been a great awakening
Of the governors of this land,
They are fighting legal battles
Against the white-robed Ku Klux Klan.

There is a governor in the southland
That is leading in the van
To stamp out the evil
Of this torturing of man.

Perhaps that "southland" governor was Arizona's progressive Governor George W. P. Hunt?

Madam Wyatt was a "dramatic reader, poetess, and enactor of plays" from Waterloo, Iowa, who performed around the country with "a repertoire second to none," said Dorothy Dix, the well-known advice columnist and social reformer. The thespian was also a friend of the Hacketts and a few years later would be their houseguest where she would be honored with a dinner.

On Saturday, December 15, 1923, the *Phoenix Tribune* reported that Dr. Hackett's practice had "one of the most modern and best equipped offices in the city." The article continued: "Dr. Hackett is the first colored physician to secure license to practice in the state of Arizona." The writer also added that the brief mention of the doctor and his success would be "unjust and absolutely unfair should we fail to accord his 'better half,' Mrs. Ayra Hackett, the credit due her. She has worked in season and out of season as a loyal, faithful wife and a loving mother to assist the Doctor in any way that she was capable . . . and is entitled to no small degree of credit for same."

In 1924, Winstona attended a new school, Eastlake Elementary, where the children used Eastlake Park as their playground. Years later Winstona still remembered the alligators that lived in the lake. Park authorities made boats available, but not surprisingly, parents were reluctant to allow their kids to paddle with the alligators. (The lake was eventually replaced with a pool.)

More worrisome was the increasing presence of the Ku Klux Klan in Phoenix. That year a Black man was severely beaten for helping a white woman step down from his shoeshine stand. Two white men, an advertising executive and a newspaper editor, were accused of the crime and tried—and then exonerated because of evidence that they might have been somewhere else at the time.

Early the next year, on February 17, 1925, tragedy struck the Hackett home that drove the headlines from their hearts. John Prentice died suddenly at age six. What caused his death has been lost to history. Ayra and Winston went on serving their community through their grief.

In 1927, the *Arizona Republican* called the Booker T. Washington Memorial Hospital "the finest and most completely equipped hospital owned and devoted to the welfare of colored people west of the Mississippi." A later ad pointed out trained nurses were in attendance night and day—and "radio connections at each patient's bed."

Black Tuesday's stock market crash hit the nation October 29, 1929, signaling the start of the Great Depression. The downturn hit the African American community especially hard—perhaps that explains why the very next month Ayra founded the *Arizona Gleam*. Eight years later, an anniversary issue of the paper said she conceived the idea to advertise the Booker T. Washington Memorial Hospital and "to help in the expansion of a great cause—the modern hospital to serve suffering humanity."

If that was indeed Ayra's goal, the paper soon expanded beyond promoting her husband's hospital into "the official organ of the Colored Citizens of Arizona."

It was the only newspaper in the state established by a female Black publisher and among a very few in the country. The staff was almost all female: Miss H. M. Fritz, RN, was associate editor, and reporters included Tillie Turner, Ruth Phillips, and Consuela McHenry. Annie Stewart reported the news from Tucson.

Even despite a competitive journalism environment, the *Gleam* did well, focusing as it did on church, biblical lessons, and school

ANNIVERSARY NUMBER

ARIZONA GLEAM

ARIZONA'S PREMIER RACE WEEKLY

VOLUME 9   PHOENIX, ARIZONA, FRIDAY, NOVEMBER 12, 1937   No. 2

BLIND MAN, FORMERLY ON RELIEF, NOW SUPPORTS FAMILY OF 13

ROXBORO, N. C., Nov. 12 (ANP) — The case of blind Percy Warnack, head of a family of 13, and a former relief client, is being cited here to show that a good man may be down, but is never out and that we get out of life just as much as we put into it. Living in Person County, Warnack, in 1933 while working on a relief project was blinded when struck by a flying stone from a dynamite blast.

Realizing the $11 a month paid him by the relief agency was not enough to support his large family, he determined to do something about it. In 1935, aided by his family he had saved $150, which he applied as a first payment on a 100-acre tract of land, being aided in his plan by Charles J. Ford, colored farm agent of the State College extension service.

During the following months, by working hard and "cutting corners wherever possible," Warnack and his family have paid $500 on their farm, hope to pay off the remaining $150 through the sale of timber. The blind man's wife is an expert canner, has put up nearly 1,000 containers of fruits and vegetables for the family larder this coming winter. Nine of Warnack's children are in school and he says he proposes to give them as good an education as possible.

Save Confessed Attacker From Detroit Mob

DETROIT, Nov. 12 (A.N.P.) — Prompt and decisive action by local authorities last Saturday night saved John S. Harris, 28, confessed attacker of a woman, from a threatened lynching, when the officers rushed Harris from Taylor Township Justice Court to a waiting auto and sped to the Detroit City Jail. A crowd of about 40 men were present at the hearing, heard the prisoner plead guilty and threatened to lynch him. He is being held under bond of $100,000 and was bound over to the Circuit Court.

SIR W. L. MARTIN
Chief Master of Pride of Arizona Temple No. 5, Knights and Daughters of Tabor, California-Arizona Jurisdiction. He is also Vice-Grand Master.

MOTORCYCLE COP SAVES CHARLESTON MAN'S LIFE

COLUMBIA, S. C., Nov 12 (ANP) — Prompt and heroic action Tuesday on the part of a Motorcyle Officer, D. R. Mc Cravey, doubtless save the life of Samuel Boston, colored resident of Charleston, when the latter's car caught fire and sprayed him with gasoline.

Boston, accompanied by several relatives, had been to State Park Hospital to visit his sister, a patient, and on the return to Charleston trouble developed in the fuel pump of his car, which he stopped to repair. When he again started the motor, the carburetor caught fire, sprayed Boston's clothing. A. L. Foster, secretary, said af which soon became a mass of flames.

Adding to his danger, Boston started to run, and at that moment, Motorcycle Policeman McCravey drove up. Grabbing the fire extinguisher from his motorcycle, he caught up with the fleeing fire victim and put out the flames, after which he rushed him to Columbia Hospital, where he was found to be seriously burned about both arms and shoulders. He

R. C. Bruce May Get Probation

NEW YORK, Nov. 12 (ANP) — A probationary sentence of 5 years may be the punishment meted out to Roscoe Conkling Bruce, the younger, when he is called to court in Newark on Wednesday, Nov. 17, to be sentenced following a guilty plea to a charge of conspiracy to defraud his former employer.

Many prominent New Jersey leaders and political figures are reported backing probation for Bruce. Among them is the First Baptist Church of Jersey City, pastored by the Rev. William A. Byrd, which recently wrote Trial Judge Brennan asking leniency, contending Bruce had been made a "goat" in the case.

Former Phoenix Resident Dies On the Coast

Mr. Webster Davis, San Diego, Calif., died on the coast last Wednesday, November 3rd, according to notices received by friends here. Mr. Davis was a former resident of Phoenix, leaving here several years ago to reside in the Coast city. Mr. Davis visited his wife Mrs. Lillian Davis and son Clarence here a few months ago.

NATIVE CHIEFS ENTERTAIN LIBERIAN PRESIDENT

MONROVIA, Nov. 12 (ANP) — Evidence of the increasing amity between the native population in Liberia and the present administration was given when the Kru population, represented by the seven chairmen of the seven tribes occupying the Borough of Kru town tendered a reception Friday to President and Mrs. Barclay. The guests included members of the cabinet, the supreme court and high officials.

N. A. A. C. P. TO MEET SUNDAY

The National Association for the Advancement of Colored People will meet Sunday afternoon at 3:30 o'clock at the C.M.E. Church, 7th Street and Jefferson.

The annual election of officers will be the important business to be transacted. 500 members are wanted at once.

NORTH CAROLINA SEEKS TO ELIMINATE "POOR HOUSES"

RALEIGH, N. C., Nov. 12 (ANP) — The County Poor House, long the logic of the aged and destitute, may be eliminated in the future, if the program sponsored by the State Department of Public Welfare is pushed to a successful conclusion. The Department seeks the ultimate elimination of county homes through substitution of Social Security Benefits, home comforts and institutional care, according to the welfare commissioner, Mrs. W. T. Bost.

Mrs. Bost pointed out this week that the State of Alabama, by giving Colley Fine

ing old people the advantage of Social Security and by consolidating welfare activities, has been able to reduce the number of county homes from 62 to 26, a decrease of more than half in one year.

Phoenix Colored People Hold Mass Meeting

Phoenix Colored Citizens held a Mass Meeting last Sunday afternoon at the Community House, 1035 Jefferson Street, for the purpose of looking into charges of reported brutality of the Phoenix Police department toward our group and to register a protest to the city authorities if the report is found to be true. A committee of 15 was appointed to look further into the matter and report at the next meeting.

More than a mile and a half of fire hose is carried on a new London fire truck constructed to serve districts where there are few hydrants.

Founder and Editor of the Arizona Gleam, the late MRS. W. C. HACKETT

Ayra Hackett, around 1935, pictured bottom right on the front page of Arizona Gleam.

Arizona Newspaper Project at the Arizona State Library, Archives and Public Records news, including sports activities ("Phoenix Monarchs Whip Sacaton Indians").

Subscription rates were $2 per year (fifty cents cheaper than the *Phoenix Tribune*), $1.25 for six months, and five cents a copy.

Home cooks could learn why they should replace butter with Crisco: "One taste of Crisco, just as it comes from the can will tell you why! Did you ever imagine a shortening could be so sweet and fresh?"

Regular columns included "The Searchlight" by Jack Truthfixer (who in one of his columns begged his readers to support the NAACP, the organization of "thinking Negroes") and the "Local and Personal" listings of which party was hosted by whom, whose cousins were visiting from where, which children were quarantined with scarlet fever, and who was late getting home from Tucson because of battery trouble.

The paper was financed by ads for local eateries, markets ("tamales and chili homemade with the finest ingredients. Orders for social affairs prepared on one day notice"), and theaters, including an announcement for the three-day showing of *Show Boat* with Paul Robeson.

Each week included an editorial just below the masthead on page 2, generally faith-based, usually penned by Ayra. The paper was also a family affair, and one March 1 edition included a poem from the next Hackett generation: "A Poem Dedicated to My Mother" by young Winstona Hackett, age twelve.

The paper occasionally had surprises, even for its editor/manager. The particular issue she refers to hasn't survived, but the Saturday, March 1, 1930, edition includes a note from Ayra:

> *The editor of The Gleam wishes to inform the public that she did not write the article that appeared in the editorial column of last week's issue of The Gleam. Neither did she see the article until it came from the press. The columns of this paper are open to receive any clean political ads regardless of party. The editor is*

*not in a position to tell you who to vote for, but I do pledge myself
to the support of the man who will give my group the fairest deal.
I am sure that regardless of what appeared in last week's editorial column, the Colored race knows who they think best to vote
for. They will vote for the man who is a friend to the Colored race.*

After three years as editor and manager, Ayra came down with
pneumonia and died suddenly on November 13, 1932, at the age of
thirty-six.

Her successor, a man named George S. Rodgers, described the
Gleam's platform as "sound and progressive; its policy fair and impar-
tial; the desire is to served [*sic*] the Colored people of Arizona and
champion the cause for better living conditions in every respect."

Rodgers put out a ninth anniversary issue of the paper and wrote
that its policy was still "to give to the readers and supporters the best
newspaper possible, and THE COOPERATION OF EVERY COL-
ORED PERSON IN THE STATE IS CORDIALLY SOLICITED."

Ayra would no doubt have been pleased to read the last paragraph
in that anniversary issue:

*The Arizona Gleam is surely and truly an Arizona newspaper. It
was born in Arizona, it lives in Arizona, it is printed in Arizona,
and is content to grow in Arizona and to help Arizona grow. As
a good Arizona citizen, are you joining in their "March of Progress" and creating a better place in which to live for yourself and
your Race?*

For the next few years Winston Hackett continued to deliver babies,
sometimes helped by Winstona, and was eventually forced by failing
eyesight and budget to close the hospital. He converted the grounds into
the Winston Inn, which welcomed Black servicemen during World War

II. In the 1949 edition of the *Negro Motorist Green Book*, the Winston Inn was the only hotel listed in all of Phoenix. Winston died in 1949.

Winstona became a teacher, married, had two children, and taught in Phoenix for many years. She died at age ninety-nine in 2017. "I still meet people my father delivered," she said in 2013. One wonders how many of them were brought into the world by Ayra Hackett.

BIBLIOGRAPHY

General References

Dobie, J. Frank. *Guide to the Life and Literature of the Southwest.* Dallas: Southern Methodist University Press, 1952.

Sheridan, Thomas E. *Arizona: A History.* Tucson: University of Arizona Press, 1995.

Lozen

Aleshire, Peter. *Warrior Woman: The Story of Lozen, Apache Warrior and Shaman.* New York: St. Martin's Press, 2001.

Ball, Eve. *In the Days of Victorio.* Tucson: University of Arizona Press, 1970.

Stockel, H. Henrietta. *Women of the Apache Nation: Voices of Truth.* Reno and Las Vegas: University of Nevada Press, 1991.

———. *Chiricahua Apache Women and Children: Safekeepers of the Heritage.* College Station: Texas A&M University Press, 2000.

———. Letter to author. August 6, 2002.

Sweeney, Edwin R. *From Cochise to Geronimo: The Chiricahua Apaches 1874–1886.* Norman: University of Oklahoma Press, 2010.

Thrapp, Dan L. *The Conquest of Apacheria.* Norman: University of Oklahoma Press, 1967.

———. *Victorio and the Mimbres Apaches.* Norman: University of Oklahoma Press, 1974.

Sister Mary Fidelia McMahon

Ames, C.S.J., Sister Aloysia. *The St. Mary's I Knew.* Tucson: St. Mary's Hospital of Tucson, Inc., 1970.

Byrne, Leo G. and Sister Alberta Cammack C.S.J. *Heritage: The Story of St. Mary's Hospital, 1880–1980.* Tucson: St. Mary's Hospital and Health Center, 1981.

McMahon, Sister Thomas Marie, C.S.J., B.A. *The Sisters of St. Joseph of Carondelet: Arizona's Pioneer Religious Congregation, 1870–1890.* Thesis presented to the Faculty of Graduate School of St. Louis University in Partial Fulfillment of the Requirements for the Degree of Master of Arts, OR, 1952. Accessed June 2, 2002, from www.library.arizona.edu/carondelet/thesis/thesis_title.html.

Quebbeman, Frances E. *Medicine in Territorial Arizona.* Tucson: Arizona Historical Foundation, 1966.

Elizabeth Hudson Smith

Cleere, Jan. "Hostess to the West." *Arizona Highways,* October 2000, 33–35.

De Graaf, Lawrence B. "Race, Sex and Region: Black Women in the American West, 1850–1920." *Pacific Historical Review,* vol. 49, no. 2, May 1980, 285–313.

Forbes, Jack D. "Black Pioneers: The Spanish-Speaking Afroamericans of the Southwest," *Phylon,* vol. 27, no. 3, Fall 1966: 233–246.

Harris, Richard E. *The First 100 Years: A History of Arizona Blacks.* Apache Junction, Arizona: Relmo Publishers, 1983.

———. *Black Heritage in Arizona.* Self-published booklet. 1977.

Katz, William Loren. *Black Women of The Old West.* New York: Atheneum, 1995.

———. *The Black West: A Documentary and Pictorial History of the African American Role in the Westward Expansion of the United States.* New York: Touchstone, 1996.

Lapp, Rudolph M. *Blacks in Gold Rush California.* New Haven: Yale University Press, 1977.

Pokorski, Doug. "Out West: Successful Female African-American Entrepreneur Had Roots Locally." *Illinois State Journal-Register* Supplement. October 12, 2001.

Ravage, John W. *Black Pioneers: Images of the Black Experience on the North American Frontier.* Salt Lake City, Utah: University of Utah Press, 1997.

Riley, Glenda. "American Daughters: Black Women in the West," chapter in Billington, Monroe Lee and Roger D. Hardaway (eds). *African Americans on the Western Frontier.* Niwot, Colorado: University Press of Colorado, 1998.

Savage, W. Sherman. *Blacks in the West.* Westport, Connecticut: Greenwood Press, 1976.

Anna E. Durkee

Adams, Bertha Snow. "A Woman Who Can Run a Mine." *Illustrated World,* September 1917, 128.

Canty, J. Michael, and Michael N. Greeley (eds). *Symposium on the History of Mining in Arizona.* Tucson, Arizona: Mining Club of the Southwest Foundation, 1988.

A History of Mining in Arizona: The Mission, Means and Memories of Arizona Miners. Accessed October 10, 2011, from www.designsbytrisha.com/Mining%20 Wrangell%20History%20No%203.pdf.

"Mistress of Twenty Says She Isn't a 'Success' Yet." *Christian Science Monitor,* June 30, 1922, 5.

Neal, Patricia A. *Mining Wrangell History: The Women of the Alaska Garnet Mining & Manufacturing Co. and the History of the Wrangell Garnet Ledge.* Accessed September 15, 2010, from www.designsbytrisha.com/Mining%20Wrangell%20 History%20No%201.pdf, www.designsbytrisha.com/Mining%20Wrangell%20 History%20No%202.pdf, and www.designsbytrisha.com/Mining%20 Wrangell%20History%20No%203.pdf.

———. Personal communication. September–October, 2011.

"Tip Gave Her a Fortune: St. Paul Woman Bought a Gold Mine and Grew Wealthy." *Los Angeles Times,* November 1916.

Tuolumne County Historical Society, California. *Timeline of History, Price and Economics of U.S. Gold.* Accessed October 16, 2011, from www.tchistory.org/ TCHISTORY/Gold_Timeline.htm.

Sharlot Mabridth Hall

Hall, Sharlot M. *Sharlot Hall on the Arizona Strip: A Diary of a Journey Through Arizona in 1911.* Prescott: Sharlot Hall Museum Press, 1999.

———. *Poems of a Ranch Woman.* Second edition. Sharlot Hall Historical Society of Arizona. Prescott, Arizona, 1989.

Maxwell, Margaret F., *A Passion for Freedom: the Life of Sharlot Hall.* Tucson & London: University of Arizona Press, 1982.

Parker, Charles Franklin. "Out of the West of Long Ago," *Arizona Highways,* January 1943, 6–11, 35.

Pearl Hart

Arizona Sentinel, Yuma, Arizona, November 25, 1899.

Boessenecker, John. *Wildcat: The Untold Story of Pearl Hart, the Wild West's Most Notorious Woman Bandit.* Toronto: Hanover Square Press, 2021.

Edwards, Harold L. "Inventing Pearl Hart." *Quarterly of the National Association for Outlaw and Lawman History, Inc.* April–June 2002, 30–37.

Hart, Pearl. "An Arizona Episode." *Cosmopolitan.* October 1899, 673–677.

Prison Records, Arizona Territorial Prison State Park, Yuma, Arizona Library: Records of Prisoner No. 1558 (Joe Boot) and No. 1559 (Pearl Hart).

Caroline Rebecca Jacobson Richardson

Anderson, J. Max. "The Polygamy Story: Fiction and Fact." Accessed October 22, 2011, from www.shields-research.org/Books/Polygamy_Story/LDS-Funde_ Polygamy_Story-c04.htm.

Denton, Sally. *Faith and Betrayal: A Pioneer Woman's Passage in the American West.* New York: Alfred A. Knopf, 2005.

Johnson, Annie Richardson. *Heartbeats of Colonia Diaz.* Shepherdsville, Kentucky: Publishers Press, 1972.

Shumway, Elva. *James and Anne Jacobson and Family.* (Family history, no date.)

Richins, Darrow and Sharon. Personal communication. May–November, 2011.

Van Wagoner, Richard S. *Mormon Polygamy: A History.* Salt Lake City: Signature Books, 1986.

"Why Do Women Choose Polygamy?: Guest Essay by an Anonymous Plural Wife." Accessed October 20, 2011, from www.principlevoices.org/our-library/essays/ why-do-women-choose-polygamy.

Teresa Urrea

Dare, Helen. "Santa Teresa, Celebrated Mexican Healer, Whose Powers Awe Warlike Yaquis in Sonora, Comes to Restore San Jose Boy to Health." The *San Francisco Weekly Examiner,* August 12, 1902.

Holden, William Curry. *Teresita.* Stemmer House Publishers: Owings Mills, Maryland, 1978.

Putnam, Frank Bishop. "Teresa Urrea, 'The Saint of Cabora.'" *Southern California Quarterly,* vol. 45, no. 3, 1963, 245–264.

Urrea, Luis. *Saint Teresita of Cabora.* Accessed March 29, 2002 from www.luisurrea .com/teres/teresita.htm.

C. Louise Boehringer

"Arizona School System is Rated Third Best in U.S.; Montana at Head of List; California Second." *Arizona Daily Star,* May 25, 1920, 8.

Boehringer, C. Louise. "Editorial Comment." *Arizona Teacher and Home Journal,* September, 1925, 6.

———. "Some Factors Making for Growth of Elementary Teachers in the Field," *The Arizona Teacher,* October 1915, 15–18.

Boehringer Clipping File, Arizona Historical Society, Tucson. "Eastern Editor Pays Tribute to Miss Boehringer," unknown newspaper, September 11, 1926.

———. "Arizona Woman is Given Honors at University of Missouri." *Arizona Republic,* October 20, 1922.

———. "A Pioneer Educator: C. Louise Boehringer, as presented by The Delta Kappa Gamma Society."

Bury, John C. *The Historical Role of Arizona's Superintendent of Public Instruction.* Vols I, II. Flagstaff, Arizona: Northern Arizona University, 1974.

Lo Vecchio, Janolyn. "C. Louise Boehringer: Arizona's First Lady of Education." Arizona Historical Society Convention Paper, April 28, 2000.

———. Personal communication. August 2002.

"Miss C. Louise Boehringer A Sure Winner." *Yuma Morning Sun,* Oct. 31, 1920.

Nilsen, Alleen Pace with Margaret Ferry and L. J. Evans (eds). *Dust in Our Desks: Territory Days to the Present in Arizona Schools.* Tempe, Arizona: Arizona State University College of Education, 1985.

Williams, E. E. "One Territorial Governor of Arizona." *Arizona Historical Review,* vol. 7, no. 1, January 1936, 71.

"Yuma Woman is Named Head of Federation of Business Clubs." *Tucson Citizen,* April 12, 1924.

Mary Kidder Rak

Rak, Mary Kidder. *A Cowman's Wife* (reprint with an introduction by Sandra L. Myres). Austin, Texas: The Texas State Historical Association, 1993.

———. *Mountain Cattle.* Boston: Houghton Mifflin Company, 1936.

Rak, Mary (Kidder) Papers, Special Collections, University of Arizona, Tucson.

Sonnichsen, C. L. *Cowboys and Cattle Kings: Life on the Range Today.* Norman: University of Oklahoma Press, 1950.

Who was Who in America, Vol. 3, pg. 708: Chicago: Marquis, 1896.

Mary-Russell Ferrell Colton

Colton, Mary-Russell F. *Art for the Schools of the Southwest: An Outline for the Public and Indian Schools.* Museum of Northern Arizona Bulletin 6. Flagstaff: Museum of Northern Arizona, 1934.

Mangum, Richard K. and Sherry G. *One Woman's West: The Life of Mary-Russell Ferrell Colton.* Flagstaff, Arizona: Museum of Northern Arizona, Northland Publishing, 1997.

Miller, Jimmy H. *The Life of Harold Sellers Colton: A Philadelphia Brahmin in Flagstaff.* Tsaile, Arizona: Navajo Community College Press, 1991.

Carmen Lee Ban

Ban, Edward, personal communication. August 20, 2002.

Editorial. *Arizona Bulletin,* July 6, 1906, 3.

Fong, Lawrence Michael. "Sojourners and Settlers: The Chinese Experience in Arizona." *Journal of Arizona History,* vol. 21, no. 3, Autumn 1980, 227–256.

Hatch, Heather (compiler). "The Chinese in the Southwest: A Photographic Record." *Journal of Arizona History,* vol. 21, no. 3, Autumn 1980, 257–274.

Hu-Dehart, Evelyn. "Immigrants to a Developing Society: The Chinese in Northern Mexico, 1875–1932." *Journal of Arizona History,* vol. 21, no. 3, Autumn 1980, 275–312.

Keane, Melissa, A.E. Rogge, Bradford Luckingham. *The Chinese in Arizona: 1870–1950 (A Component of the Arizona Historic Preservation Plan).* Phoenix: Arizona Historic Preservation Office, 1992.

The Promise of Gold Mountain: Tucson's Chinese Heritage. Accessed July 15, 2002, from www.library.arizona.edu/Images/chamer/railroad_041801.html.

Tom, Mike L. Personal communication. August 2002.

Polingaysi Qöyawayma

History of the Hopi People. Accessed July 31, 2002, from www.hopi.nsn.us/Pages/ History/history.html.

Norwood, Vera and Janice Monk, eds. *The Desert Is No Lady: Southwestern Landscapes in Women's Writing and Art.* New Haven: Yale University Press, 1987; Tucson: University of Arizona Press.

Qöyawayma, Polingaysi (Elizabeth Q. White). *No Turning Back: A Hopi Woman's Struggle to Live in Two Worlds* (as told to Vada B. Carlson). Albuquerque: University of New Mexico Press, 1964.

———. Arizona Women's Hall of Fame. Phoenix, 1991.

———. Biography included in Native North American pages of the African Americans Publications website. Accessed July 31, 2002, from www.nativepubs.com/ nativepubs/Apps/bios/0510QoyawaymaPolingaysi.asp?pic_none.

Luisa Ronstadt Espinel

Griffith, Jim. "The Singing Ronstadts and *Canciones de Mi Padre:* A Musical Family." Accessed August 29, 2002, from www.library.arizona.edu/images/ronstadt/music/ cancintr.html.

Gutierrez, Ana B. "Luisa Espinel: Another Ronstadt Family Superstar." *Tucson Citizen,* October 12, 1985.

"Lovely Dream, Reviewer Calls Espinel Songs." *Tucson Citizen,* November 11, 1927.

"Luisa Espinal [sic] Has High Honor." *Arizona Daily Star,* April 25, 1928.

"Luisa Espinel's Love of Tucson Told in a Sketch." *Arizona Daily Star,* December 3, 1933.

"Miss Louise Ronstadt Writes of Her Experiences in Spain." *Tucson Citizen,* December 20, 1925.

Rochlin, Harriet. "Brides for Brethren: Arizona Territory, 1854–1883." Accessed August 24, 2002, from www.rochlin-roots-west.com/author_brides.htm.

Ronstadt, Federico José María. *Borderman: The Memoirs of Federico José María Ronstadt.* Accessed August 28, 2002, from www.library.arizona.edu/images/ ronstadt/bordermn/.html.

Ronstadt, Luisa Espinel Papers, Arizona Historical Society, Tucson, Arizona.

Sheridan, Thomas E. *Los Tucsonenses: The Mexican Community in Tucson, 1854–1941.* Tucson: University of Arizona Press, 1986.

Sonnichsen, C. L. *Tucson: The Life and Times of an American City.* Norman: University of Oklahoma Press, 1982.

Sara Plummer Lemmon

Agnew, Brad, and Kelly Agnew. *John Gill Lemmon: Andersonville Survivor and California Botanist*. Dan Bernardino: Kindle Direct, 2020.

Brown, Wynne. *The Forgotten Botanist: Sara Plummer Lemmon's Life of Science and Art*. Lincoln: University of Nebraska Press, 2021.

Lemmon, J. G. "A Botanical Wedding Trip." *The Californian, a Western Monthly Magazine* 4 (July–December 1881): 512.

Lemmon, Sara Plummer. Letters and Ephemera: Martha Everett St. John and Harold St. John Collection of Sara Plummer and John Gill Lemmon Material. University and Jepson Herbaria, University of California, Berkeley.

Laura Kerman

Lindauer, Owen. "Archeology of the Phoenix Indian School." Archaeology.org. March 27, 1998. archive.archaeology.org/online/features/phoenix/.

Nabhan, Gary Paul. *The Desert Smells Like Rain: A Naturalist in O'odham Country*. Tucson: University of Arizona Press, 1982.

Reichhardt, Karen. Personal communication. January–June 2022.

Reichhardt, Karen Louise. "Before We Knew the Years Had Numbers: The Memoirs of Laura Kerman, Tohono O'odham Woman." *Journal of the Southwest* 61, no. 3 (Autumn 2019): 437–549.

Ayra Hackett

Arizona Memory Project. The *Arizona Gleam* collection. Accessed January 21, 2022. azmemory.azlibrary.gov/digital/collection/theazgleam.

———. The *Phoenix Tribune* collection. Accessed January 27, 2022. azmemory .azlibrary.gov/digital/collection/phxtribune/id/1473/.

Pratcher, Anthony, II. Personal communication. October 2021.

Talton, Jon. "Phoenix 101: Minorities." *Rogue Columnist*, November 5, 2009. roguecolumnist.com/rogue_columnist/2009/11/phoenix-101-minorities.html.

Whitaker, Matthew. Personal communication. January 2022.

———. "The Rise of Black Phoenix: African-American Migration, Settlement and Community Development in Maricopa County, Arizona 1868–1930." *Journal of Negro History* 85, no. 3 (2000): 197–209.

INDEX

ABOUT THE AUTHOR

Wynne Brown is a freelance writer/editor/graphic designer based in Tucson on the Arizona lands of the Tohono O'odham Nation and the Pascua Yaqui Tribe. Her most recent book is *The Forgotten Botanist: Sara Plummer Lemmon's Life of Science and Art* (2021). She is also the author of *The Falcon Guide to Trail Riding Arizona* and the coeditor *of Cave Creek Canyon: Revealing the Heart of Arizona's Chiricahua Mountains.* All her books have won a wide variety of regional and national awards.

Wynne has worked as a scientific illustrator in addition to spending six years as a reporter and copyeditor at a midsize daily newspaper. She is also the president of Chiricahua Regional Council, the Pima County representative to the State Board of the Arizona Historical Society, and was the spring 2022 Pima County Public Library writer in residence.

Her website is wynnebrown.com.